MY H
BURNED
AND
NOW I CAN SEE
THE STARS

Reflections on
Losing and Finding

ANN HISLE

DOVER PUBLICATIONS, INC.
Mineola, New York

Bibliographical Note

My House Burned Down and Now I Can See the Stars is a new work,
first published by Dover Publications, Inc., in 2015.

International Standard Book Number
ISBN-13: 978-0-486-79496-9
ISBN-10: 0-486-79496-2

Manufactured in the United States by RR Donnelley
79496202   2015
www.doverpublications.com

For
John
and our children
Christine, Beth, David, and Peter
and their families
with love

ACKNOWLEDGMENTS

For so many generous and good people who have shared their time and wisdom with me, I feel so appreciative and thank God. I begin with Diana Hanssen, my treasured college friend and editor. She went through the entire manuscript with me and asked me to clarify some sentences, add on to others, and put brackets in the middle of other sentences to describe the storyteller's actions. We sighed, empathized, and laughed together many evenings—she was/is an invaluable gift. Mike Slattery was another dear friend and editor, particularly for the Introduction. Jim Miller, my editor at Dover Publications, could not have been more easy-going, open, and approachable; yet another gift for this new author. M. C. Waldrep was also incredibly open—she was my first contact at Dover Publications and agreed to look at the manuscript of a fledgling author who had no agent. Thank you, M. C. And then there were all those friends and acquaintances who so willingly read the work and were encouraging. They often let me know what stories they loved, liked, or didn't appreciate as much. Thank you Marilyn Chandler McEntyre, Reggie Morales, Melanie Weiland, Lynn Mattingly, Judith Reuter, Lilyan Dickerson, Dave Cavanagh, Annilee Openheimer, Tony Tombasco, Ginn Goldsmith, Joanne Littlefair, Carolyn Mandell, Gail Mandell, Mary Carol Dragoo, Jane Coe, Jean Chandler, Sally Bosken, Marie France, Sandra El-Khodary, Sara Perry, Joanne Springer, Rosemary Shiner, Diana Ruth, Rose Mazur, Michael Newton, Bob Neuman, and Jeanne Castro.

Finally, there would be no book if it weren't for my faithful, loving, patient, teasing husband of almost fifty years. Thank you, John, for unscrambling all my computer glitches, reading over innumerable sentences or quotes, and, most significantly, for being my loving life companion through all our losings and findings. What joy to look at and for the stars with you.

PHOTO CREDITS

With thanks for the gift of images to accompany the meditation quotes to Susan Robbins Etherton, McLean, Virginia, www.susanrobbinsetherton.zenfolio.com. A photographer for the transformative Shalem Institute for Spiritual Formation in Washington, DC, Susan generously offered choices from her many creative and beautiful photographs and greeting cards. The photos in chapters 2, 3, 4, 5, 8, 9, and 11 are all hers.

Additional thanks to John Pontius for the chapter 1 photo, Jean Johnson for the chapter 7 photo, and John Hisle for the photos in chapters 6 and 10.

CONTENTS

Chapters/ Practices:

Each chapter discusses a waking-up spiritual practice to expand our **CONSCIOUSNESS.**

Each chapter furthers the thesis that we need to lose in order to find.

Each chapter shares at least one story of hope, of a person seeing with new eyes—seeing freshly.

The book invites the reader to do the same.

INTRODUCTION

Tomorrow, today is gone. An intrinsic part of daily life is losing: whether it be the loss of our temper, the irritating loss of our car keys, or the heartbreaking loss of a beloved parent. However, on the other side of these losses it is possible, eventually, to make an active, deliberate choice—to find a way to be less reactive, a place for a spare set of keys, a way to be closer to our remaining parent.

When we are ready to look, we notice that both "losing" and "finding" are complementary to each other and fundamental to life. In fact, they're holding hands. When we lose anything, we gradually learn that the loss is not the end of the story.

Significant loss or significant perceived loss sends most of us headlong into shock, into the *underneathness* of life. It is there in the depths that we often question what really matters and learn some life lesson, such as: control is an illusion, we are all vulnerable. With one telephone call, our planned life can dramatically change.

My planned life changed when I was seventeen. My mother received a call—her biopsy revealed advanced lymphoma cancer. The impact of her diagnosis and her death less than a year later was profound. My mother's religious faith and my father's philosophy of "stiff upper lip" prepared me to a degree. However, it took years to really absorb the deep impact of losing my mom, and a few years later my only aunt, and twenty years later my dad, all to cancer. My parents' deaths would influence many of my choices, one of which was to become a bereavement counselor.

As a bereavement counselor and psychotherapist for over thirty-five years, I have had the privilege to accompany many people coming to terms with heart-wrenching loss. I have observed that their healing arises out of a willingness to "break open" and ask deeper questions about life's mysteries. Their healing arises out of a willingness to keep hope alive. A carefully nurtured and practiced attitude of hope can transfigure the very landscape of our lives. With hope, we can see that the dead and dry seeds in the barren fields of winter paradoxically contain abundant life.

How do we nurture and practice this attitude of hope? Well, we might choose to act with hope and make a habit of it! We live in possibility. We can choose to look with fresh eyes at whatever we experience—out of the mud, lotus flowers grow.

So, as we weep over losing a loved one or a fire-ravaged house, we can mindfully choose to "be with" the loss and hopefully look beyond the ashes to the light of the stars. Little by little we can accept our grieving as part of the universal flow of living. We can hold the loneliness and the missing in the one hand, and the cherished memories and new experiences in the other hand. As we move through life's stages, adapting to wanted and unwanted changes, we carry with us some hurt and fear, *as well as* hope and peace. While we cannot insulate ourselves from the unwanted changes, we can prepare ourselves for them, to a degree.

Embracing the spiritual practices suggested in the following chapters helps us to prepare and to more consciously participate in the flow of our life story. These chapters—this book—is for everyone who has faced the pain of losing. And, is that not all of us? It is for everyone who is open to seeing from a new perspective and exploring certain practices that can become second nature, even habit. These practices are like water enlivening the seeds within all of us—enabling us to be green once again. Most worthwhile pursuits require "showing up" and practice. Some practices are physical, such as regularly playing the guitar and exercising with weights. Other practices are spiritual, often flowing from chosen attitudes of humility, hopefulness, and gratitude. These practices are not only the foundation of this book, but also the foundation of remarkable awakenings that lead us to deeper living, deeper loving, deeper humanity—they can transform our hearts.

PREFACE

In the following pages I attempt to share spiritual practices that have significantly influenced my and others' adult life. I grew up in the Christian tradition with a Catholic mother and Lutheran father. During college years, I broadened my interests and studied Quakerism, Judaism, and Buddhism.

As my journey continued, I discovered that at the root of whatever the spiritual tradition I studied was a simple and profound injunction: to love your neighbor as yourself. Live compassionately toward everyone and everything under and with the God of our understanding.

We need daily practices—applicable in every tradition—to help move us out of our own self-preoccupation into the bigger and closer family of humankind. It is my hope that the pages ahead encourage this movement.

"The most important question facing humanity is, 'Is the universe a friendly place?' This is the first and most important question all people must answer for themselves."

—Albert Einstein, scientist

"If I flew to the point of sunrise, or westward across the sea,
Your hand would still be guiding me,
Your right hand holding me."

—Psalm 139: 9-10

CHAPTER 1

Playing with Paradox and Irony

An old clay Buddha statue had been a time-honored treasure in Thailand for millennia. My "English as a Second Language" student from Thailand told me that over many years slight cracks gradually deepened and pure gold was found underneath the statue's exterior. Unknown to anyone, the clay exterior was just a protective covering over a pure gold Buddha which had been hidden for centuries. My student smiled: "We don't all the time see."

When we humbly recognize our sometime-blindness, we open to mystery, surprise and irony. Playing around with and being open to irony is a rich spiritual practice.

We do know, but often forget, that the feared and resisted move to Chicago can—ironically—become, just a year later, "the best thing that could have happened to our family." The devastating birth of a Special Needs child can become a family's great blessing. And the outcast can become "the Good Samaritan." "We don't all the time see," or understand. An open, almost playful, "who knows" posture invites an openness to and a "wondering-about" what's around the corner.

Opposites do not necessarily oppose one another. Indeed, opposites regularly need and complement one another. We may have first learned about the connectedness of opposites, non-duality, in the wonderful games of peek-a-boo and hide-and-go-seek. Absence and presence are holding hands. Daddy's presence is taken for granted, but once he hides, his presence is cherished. We lose our power during a winter storm and when the heat and light return, we are electric with joy. Do we have to lose something before we *really* find it? The losing and finding in these

3

simple childhood games can be a metaphor for our life journey of losing and seeking, seeking and finding, finding and appreciating.

Marlene's loss of good health was initially "bad news, bad luck, bad everything"—an enveloping dark cloud prevented any light from reaching her. However, frustrated by the irritation, worry, resentment, and ever-present cloud in her daily life, she began searching for something more.

She found a "One Day at a Time" support group and began feeling less devastated and more empowered and motivated. It was at this time that she visited her daughter on the West coast. En route home, she noticed me and my husband walking back and forth in the airport while we waited for our plane. She subsequently boarded the same airplane with us for Washington, D.C., and happened to sit in front of us. Marlene spontaneously turned around to face us and mentioned that she had been inspired out of her sad and lonely feelings when she had noticed us walking before "take-off." She told us: "I too started walking—I lately walk and talk myself into better moods."

We chatted about our respective visits to the Santa Fe area. I commented that while in Taos I had accidentally run into the man who initially hired me for Hospice work in Washington, D.C.

Marlene responded:

"This is unbelievable. You are the only person I have spoken to since leaving my daughter and just the person I need. I have terminal cancer and I came last week to Santa Fe to personally tell my daughter about a metastasis. She just dropped me off at the airport and got lost on the way here—she's beside herself with worry and also already busy managing my care. Her parting words were, 'Mom, promise me to find some kind of grief counselor to help you with your cancer and other losses.' And about one hour after I left her I met you and you *just happen* to be a grief counselor. How amazing is that?

"My smart daughter told me that nothing alive was static and challenged me to keep being alive till I'm not. All her suggestions were beginning to exhaust me—-she worked hard to show me she could, we could ... we would get through this together and get help when needed."

Marlene was eager to share her story. She reflected:

"As I tire more readily and try to orchestrate situations less, more serendipitous gifts seem to come my way. My slowed-down mornings allow for time to pay attention to the gift of dreams. While in Santa Fe, I dreamt I was standing in my grandmother's vast vegetable garden teaching a course, 'Don't Just Do Something, Sit There.' Watching with wide-open eyes has become more and more of a cure for me as I gradually am accepting the terminal nature of my diagnosis. I sense a mysterious, profound soul-confidence and a decreasing hunger for others' approval. I initially felt free to thrash around in the dark with my anger, with my feelings of unfairness, and with my isolation, because deep down I had unacknowledged faith. [I thought to myself: deep down there was pure gold.] I had faith that somehow I'd 'get-through' things. [She stopped and smiled] It's quite remarkable ... as I stop fighting what I can't change; things seem to change. ... As I let go of striving for the *right* thing to say, the *right* haircut, the right gift, I can relax and enjoy what simply comes my way. ... Rich is how much you can do without."

On the plane I mentioned to Marlene that she seemed *both* exhausted *and* empowered, sad *and* joyful right then as we talked. A couple of weeks after returning home Marlene, again eager to talk, phoned me, saying:

"I'm getting it. I'm feeling independent and strong by my reading, centering prayer, and my 'One Day At A Time' support group. At the same time I'm feeling dependent on friends and on doctors for my chemotherapy treatments and at times am damn scared and tired. I'm restless and peaceful, I'm selfish and generous, I'm fearful and confident—all in the same day. I'm full of weeds and wheat. It's not the losses or the conflict that has been my problem; it's been my avoiding of conflict that has too often deadened my spirit [long pause here]. ... I agree with you, creative tension is mandatory. My wonderful friend reminded me that a beautiful pearl is formed by the irritation of a grain of sand in the oyster, and grapes must ferment before there is fine wine. I'm opening to the natural cycles of life and so much more appreciative and amazed by the rhythms of life all around me, in me ... for me. Nothing is static. I want to terminate my overwhelming preoccupation with myself and live bigger [again, a long pause and some deep breathing]. Sitting by my front window and watching children daily return from school now is great theater. I was so happy when I saw my neighbor's child stop a bully from throwing dandelion weeds at an awkward often-alone young boy. ... Ultimately my soft dying will be my final gift to God and my daughter and maybe even my ex. Since death's visit is closer and closer, I appreciate even a sneeze. I no longer rush—I don't have that kind of time. When I'm in my accepting mode [and here, she had a soft laugh], I'm kind of living in heaven or luminous space right now. I feel light, I'm bathed in Light, Light is in me. Oh, my God, thank you for the time, for the Process of my slowly letting go of the junk—all my worrying, my fears, my grasping. ... Rich *is* appreciating how much you can live without."

Marlene read that many dying patients report having dreams about some sort of journey, whether by foot, train, or mule cart. Additionally, many such patients have had visits in their dreams from deceased relatives or friends. Marlene decided to keep a journal of her dreams and was thrilled that my Hospice experiences corroborated her reading and her experience. The veil between life and death was thinner and thinner.

During the five years between her life-threatening diagnosis and her death, Marlene was *both* awakefully dying *and* awakefully living. She was vulnerable and resilient. As she became weaker physically, she awakened to the peaceful silence underneath all the sounds of life surrounding her. While on oxygen the last days of her life, she scribbled: "I cry to leave here *and* my heart is filled with ___." She drew a light bulb.

Inspired by Marlene and others like her, I often ask clients to play with this "Both-And" concept. Here are some of their responses:

"I was upset that my old air conditioner broke down, *and* now am glad I can better hear the birds, wake up in good fresh air, save on my energy bill, and am not blasted by heat every time I go outside."

"I was truly devastated upon becoming blind at age of twenty-six, *and* now at age thirty-five I am thankful for my blindness. I can not only hear, smell, and feel better, but *see* better. I was so distracted—blinded—by outer appearances that I never experienced all the light and life right inside of me."

"I'm both frustrated that my car is in the repair shop *and* happy that I'm now getting the exercise that my doctor ordered for my diabetes … and am more environmentally friendly."

"My divorce was both absolutely horrible *and* over time an opportunity for new behaviors. Now I am less bossy and have a much deeper relationship with two of our three grown children."

"As I grow older, acquaintances and friends of mine are sick and dying, *but* I'm so much more appreciative of my daily living."

"Both/and" qualities of life are continually dancing together all over the place: the tide receding and returning, the sun setting and rising, the acorn dying and the tree growing.

I particularly appreciate the "hand-holding" of *both* contemplation *and* action (humble listening and active participation). I can appreciate the African proverb: When you pray, move your feet. The God of my understanding invites Sabbath time, still time to humbly withdraw from the world and be *in* the presence of the extraordinary in the ordinary; *and* my God invites empowered "feet-moving," "seeking-justice," "loving-tenderly," "walking-humbly" action as I participate in the world.

Jesus suggests this balancing connection in the New Testament, in Matthew 10:39. Jesus declares that it is in yielding ourselves (losing our self-absorbed, controlling, competing, comparing false self) that we find ourselves (our generous, creative, loving true self). Most of Jesus' teaching parables are paradoxical, and several are about losing and finding—a lost sheep, a lost coin, a lost son. In John 12:24 we are further taught: "unless a grain of wheat falls to the ground and dies, it remains just a grain of wheat; but if it dies it produces much fruit." Poet Mark Nepo adds:

"All the buried seeds
crack open in the dark
the instant they surrender
to a process they can't see."

Marlene surrendered to a mysterious internal process. She came to agree with thirteenth-century mystic Meister Eckhart that healthy living was much more about subtraction than addition. She became a noticer—a noticer of irony. "I had to empty out, let go of so much to see what real life was bubbling forth from within. I'm now a noticer of goodness," she pronounced. "I've lost my negativity—well, decreased it! " What if she had chosen only to focus on herself and her cancer?

When our focus is more narrow and we are cut off from the wide expanse of the stars, it is a disaster. Isn't it interesting that the etymology of the word *disaster* is: *dis*-away from; *astro*-star? To be away from the starry mysterious heavens is soul-killing, is disaster.

Indeed in embracing the larger life-story as it presents itself, we may, along with author Reinhold Niebuhr, hope to mysteriously have "the serenity to accept what we cannot change, the courage to change what we can, and the wisdom to know the difference." Actor Michael J. Fox mysteriously accepted what he could not change. On a June 2012 episode of *Frontline*, he shared that Parkinson's Disease helped him ask questions he never would have asked. He said he wouldn't want to go back to when he was pre-Parkinson's: "While I have a loss, I have much more … better to look at the better part of what exists as a way of potential rather than bad as dominant reality."

We can learn from the Buddhists who suggest we all have 10,000 sufferings and 10,000 joys, each complimenting the other. Playing with paradox, we may see we need our physical limitations *and* our physical abilities; our crosses *and* resurrections; our need for contemplation *and* for action; our need for rainy days *and* for sunny days; and, finally, our need for conditional love *and* unconditional love. All of it together.

FOR MEDITATION

Playing with Paradox

"... So the soft and supple are the companions of life
While the stiff and unyielding are the companions of death."
—Lao Tzu, author of *Tao Te Ching*, 500 B.C.

"It is a good thing to have all the props pulled out from under us occasionally. It gives us some sense of what is rock under our feet and what is sand."
—Madeleine L'Engle, author

"Stillness is what creates Love
Movement is what creates Life.
To be still
Yet still moving—
That is everything."

—Do Hyun Choe, Sufi Master

"When we no longer know what to do,
we have come to our real work,
and when we no longer know which way to go,
we have begun our journey.
The mind that is not baffled is not employed.
The impeded spring is the one that sings."

—Wendell Berry, poet

"A Chinese farmer had a horse that ran off.
He said to his neighbor, "What bad luck I have."

The neighbor said, "Bad luck, good luck, who knows?"
The next day, the horse returned, over the hill with five wild stallions and
the farmer said, "What good luck I have."

The neighbor said, "Good luck, bad luck, who knows?"
The farmer's son, in attempting to train the stallions, was thrown and broke
his leg. The farmer again said, "What bad luck I have."

The neighbor said, "Bad luck, good luck, who knows?"
The next week, militia from the neighboring village came to conscript all
young men for war and the farmer said, "What good luck I have, my son
will not be able to go."

The neighbor said, "Good luck, bad luck, who knows?"
—"The Chinese Farmer," an old Zen tale.

CHAPTER 2

Acknowledging Our Suffering

When I did my School of Social Work field-placement, I worked with Jerome, a grieving four-year-old. His father had recently died from a tragic work-related accident at a construction site. Jerome acknowledged his pain, cried daily, and consistently begged me to make a home visit after pre-school. His home was full of absence. Jerome responded. At his apartment, Jerome repeatedly acted out the "Humpty Dumpty" nursery rhyme. It had been read to him in our federally funded Pre-K program for at-risk children. He always asked me to read about Humpty Dumpty falling off the wall. Then he play-acted falling off the chair and asked me to help wrap him "back together again" in toilet paper.

Jerome had a "conversation" with his suffering. He allowed and acknowledged his pain by searching for meaning, companionship, and healing—a spiritual practice.

He seemed to metaphorically look for a flashlight or candle rather than just curse the darkness. Hoping to feel better, he humbly responded to an inner prompting—he "conversed" with the mystery of his vulnerable, anxious feelings. He was healing. He connected with another broken creature who gave him hope. Humpty and he could be put back together. Jerome gradually moved from wrapping himself to wrapping a ripped pet monkey, and eventually to interest in other things. Something within, a grace, inspired this creative and life-affirming response. There are other responses. Jerome could have become angry or numb; he could have fought with his mother and others about the reality of his dad's death. He could have denied the death and the fearful emotions accompanying

11

the loss of his special parent. He could have become negative, depressed, and dark.

Poet Emily Dickinson wrote: "We grow accustomed to the Dark—When Light is put away— ..." Jerome and Lisa McFarland, a young woman with whom I worked in therapy, both struggled *not* to put Light away. Like Jerome, Lisa also wrestled and dealt with her raw feelings of hollowness, loneliness, and gut-wrenching pain. She wrote this reflection:

"Our only daughter Alexis died four years ago at age 13 months. Her life and death have impacted my life in numerous ways, both joyous and painful. I never knew how deeply I could love, or how empty I could feel, until she came to us.

"The decision to let Alexis go did not come easily. We fought long and hard for quality of life for her. Months in the hospital, nurses and technology in our home, and several medical specialists could not provide her a life without suffering. Simultaneously, her body failed her, and it was no longer our decision to make. She was finally at peace. We were not.

"I fell to the floor as her lifeless infant body was taken from my arms, leaving them empty for the first time since her birth. I was devastated. Breathless, I tried to imagine my life without her. I could not. Over the days, weeks, and months that followed, I was unable to move. I felt as if time had stopped. I was offended at the rising of the sun each morning. How could the world still be turning? I felt I would not survive without her.

"Lost and bottomed out, I began the ongoing process of grief work. I stopped running from what I felt. I let it in, slowly. I talked to people who would listen. I went to therapy. I wrote down my feelings. I sat quietly in Alexis's bedroom. I daydreamed. I spent time with people who love me. I cried. I cried. I cried. I still cry.

"Now, four years later I work in a career that honors her life. I am a pediatric intensive care nurse. My marriage is strong. We are raising our two-year-old son and we just bought our very first home.

"I don't know when my hope for life was restored. Maybe it was when our son was born. Maybe it was when I became a pediatric nurse. Maybe it was when I really belly-laughed again for the first time. Or maybe it was when that butterfly flew into my car at the cemetery.

"But there is hope. Sometimes it means getting through the hour. Sometimes it is daring to dream. Sometimes it is looking at someone in a new way, or taking a very deep breath of fresh air. Perhaps it is a very inspiring sunrise. Because, as I have learned, that stubborn sun does rise, like it or not. And when it does, a new day has begun. Hope shines its light on each of us. Only we can decide how to live in it."

Lisa sat down with her feelings, gradually accepted her emptiness, and gradually and mysteriously hope and joy returned.

Lisa's attitude reminds me of theologian and paleontologist Teihard de Chardin, S.J., who wrote:

"Do not brace yourself against suffering.
Try to close your eyes and surrender yourself,
As if to a great loving energy.
This attitude is neither weak nor absurd.
It is the only one that cannot lead us astray.
Try to 'sleep' with the active sleep of confidence
Which is that of the seed in the fields of winter."

Centuries ago, the Chinese people realized this truth: Do not resist suffering. If suffering is given space and "chewed on," it eventually has a gift, a teaching that becomes sweet. The Chinese characters for the word suffering are translated: "eat bitter melon soup." To this day, when Chinese bitter melon is chewed on, it becomes sweet.

Jews discuss this concept: Jonah's shipwreck and capture by a whale precedes his finding freedom for himself and the Ninevites. Christians also: Good Friday leads to Easter Sunday—Jesus's dying leads to new life. In the secular world, athletes discuss this journey: simply, no pain, no gain.

Children whose broad emotional life has been accepted and nourished often respond to suffering without much hesitation—they are wide awake to what is happening in their internal and external worlds. They can "chew on" their uncomfortable feelings. Years ago when our daughter Christine's grandfather died, her thirteen-year-old friend Kate Silverstein, who loved poetry, explored sorrow by writing this poem:

"When I saw you last, you were old and tired.
Lying mouth open, next to a table cluttered with bottles of life.
And yet—I remember you before and even during your illness,
as a kind, gentle man.
You've made me regret that I have never in my life gotten
to love my Grandfather.
My jealousy of your family was great . . . how I longed to call you Papa.
You were not a saint, and yet—you helped in the creation of someone
very close to me.
You made me scared of what lies beyond life.
You made me fear the persistent, clutching hands of death.
Yet—you showed me a kind of courage I will not soon forget."

Grace was an equally open child. She, upon hearing of her surrogate grandfather's death, spontaneously ran across the street to be with her Grandma Amey—she sought the comfort of connection. Grace's mother followed her several minutes later and was dumbfounded when she found Grace simply sitting still next to Grandma Amey, holding her hand. Grace's mom quietly backed away and returned home. Grace later told her mom that Grandma Amey had told her Grandpa Amey stories, shown her a few old photos, and then they had some lemon cookies.

And finally, a third inspiring child, Dahlia, acknowledged her suffering and found a way to healing. After a parents' support group at the "Pre-K" program, a few mothers were discussing the significance of pets in their early lives. Dahlia walked me back to my office and told me this story about her youth:

"A cat saved my life when I was in third grade. Well, a librarian and a cat. You know my mom drank a lot and usually had a flavor-of-the-month boyfriend over at night, and I was all alone in the back bedroom apartment.

I was lonely and scared when they got into fights and I would talk to my two stuffed animals about my mom's fighting. Then Miss Marjorie comes into the picture. She was the school librarian who noticed I cried during one of her stories—I remember, it was about an orphan mountain girl. She paid me special attention and, as summer vacation was coming, asked if I would be allowed to have a cat. My mom said no but she changed her mind a few days later. I found out later Miss Marjorie talked again to my mom. The cat I named Juniper became my best friend. She jumped on my lap when I got home from school and at bedtime she purred me to sleep *and* she listened to me cry, to my day's stories, and to all my make-believe tales. Juniper was my only 'real' friend till 6th grade when Samantha from Scotland moved into my building."

Suffering is a part of life that asks us to stop and struggle with the feelings associated with it. The pain of suffering keeps introducing and re-introducing us to our true selves from cradle to grave. Profound loss, resulting in stop-everything-grief, often provokes despair, crippling anxiety, and sometimes rage. Profound loss often invites us to ask bigger questions: How can I survive, thrive? What holds my life together? Can I accept that over which I have no control? Am I suffering because I cannot face losing control? What gives meaning to my life? When *I* die what will *my* legacy be?

Ignoring or denying the pain only exacerbates the hurt. As Merlin, in *The Once and Future King*, says: "When you're sad, the only thing to do is learn something." Jerome's, Lisa's and Dahlia's feelings of desolation were acknowledged and contemplated—the healing and learning process could begin. They were present to pain and absence.

Those persons who choose to grieve by questioning and adapting to the painful and lonely reality of an empty chair, a job loss, a spouse's death can thrive. They realize suffering is basic to life but misery is not. They *both* feel the ache *and* hold hope for a finding. They search for a new door to open after a doorway to a place of love has been closed. Remarkably, they find a way *and* mysteriously and amazingly, a way finds them.

FOR MEDITATION
Acknowledging Our Suffering

"Life is difficult, but once we accept that life is difficult, it is not so difficult."

—M. Scott Peck, M.D., author

"What will determine the course of your life more than any one thing is whether or not you're willing to tolerate necessary discomfort."

—Barbara Sher, psychologist, author

"It is well known that emotions of the soul affect the body and produce great, significant and wide-ranging changes in the state of health. Emotions of the soul (feelings) should be watched, regularly examined, and kept in balance."

—Maimonides, 12th century sage

"Pain is a small price to pay for freedom from self-delusion."

—David Steindl-Rast, theologian, author

The Guest House

"This being human is a guest house.
Every morning is a new arrival.
A joy, a depression, a meanness,
some momentary awareness comes
as an unexpected visitor.

Welcome and entertain them all!
Even if they're a crowd of sorrows,
who violently sweep your house
empty of its furniture,
still treat each guest honorably.
He may be cleaning you out for some new delight.
The dark thought, the shame, the malice,
meet them at the door laughing,
and invite them in.
Be grateful for whoever comes,
because each has been sent
as a guide from beyond."

—Mawlana Jalal al-Din Rumi,
13th century Sufi poet

CHAPTER 3

Sharing Our Story

Dana had been feeling particularly lonely and sad. It was her recently deceased husband's birthday. She pushed herself to get out of the house and go to the cemetery. After sitting at the gravesite for a while, she offered her sentiments to her deceased spouse and, as she was leaving, felt compelled to quietly sing "Happy Birthday." She later related to me that, as she sang, several Hispanic gravediggers spontaneously stopped their work, took off their straw hats, put their hats on their hearts, and bowed their heads in community. This gentle gesture of respect led Dana to see loss more as a universal experience rather than simply an individual grief. Dana felt a common bond not only with the Hispanic men whom she had never seen before but with everybody. At our Hospice office, she later enthusiastically told me:

"Maybe separation is an illusion ... maybe everything is interconnected, as I'm learning in my Ecology Continuing Ed Class. My teacher told us even hermit crabs need company and connection—left alone, crabs suffer deteriorating health and may even lose a claw or leg."

Since the beginning of recorded history, humans have gathered into some form of group and shared stories—this spiritual practice encourages sharing vulnerability, listening with head *and* heart, and trusting.

Exchanging tales helps us make sense of our lives and connect one with another. The story character, whether mythical or not, can reveal deeper aspects of ourselves that are beautiful and less than beautiful. A person seems like a match that can "exist by itself" but when it connects with flint, there's fire. We can be "flint"—perhaps encouraging a shy person to go on a blind date, encouraging a "burned-out" colleague to try for a new job, encouraging an oft-fatigued friend to ask some questions, seek medical attention or explore a healthier lifestyle. Another person can not only re-introduce us to ourselves, but also invite us into uncharted territory. We need this other person *both* to help us know ourselves *and* to help us move beyond ourselves. And this other person needs the same helping from us.

When my exhausted care-taking friend returned to school one Monday after spring break, her fellow teachers helped her to reconnect with herself and others. She wrote to me:

"Gathered around the lunch table at work this week, separation between me and my colleagues collapsed. I broke down while I was telling them about Mike's autoimmune disease. I felt connected by nods of agreement, a name remembered, listening ears. It seems as if my opening inspired some others to tell their story of loss or challenge. Unbelievably, a few of us met for coffee again early Saturday to continue; we were hungry to know each other better. The new second-grade teacher had cared for her husband with Lou Gehrig's disease for two years while teaching to support her two children in college. We weren't trying to out-suffer each other, but we realized that misery does love some company and that everyone has visits with suffering. … We left each other each time with good tears and hugs. I wonder if this is because we're all elementary-school teachers and so involved with kids' emotions?"

Bruce, a grief group participant, was the caring connection that helped his wife Hillary open up. Bruce shared their story with the grief group:

"After Hillary's diagnosis of ovarian cancer and our period of adjusting to the traumatic news, we made more time for real conversations rather than sound bites. I probed Hillary's edginess and Hillary, eventually trusting my caring, became more communicative of her fears. Over many cups of peppermint and licorice tea Hillary revealed her shame for feeling so anxious and obsessed with her worries ... for not being as courageous and spiritual as some other cancer patients getting chemotherapy. She talked and she wept and she talked some more. She noticed how much living could come about by discussing what really mattered—being present with love to whoever was near. She calmed and began to sleep better and even agreed to talk to our old pastor. She responded to our pastor's suggestion of reminiscing and even imagining life without each other. We followed pastor Gerry's lead. Hillary said she would miss my playfulness, loving touch ... my presence. I said I would miss her loving presence, her tender mothering, and even her opinions—take smaller bites, slow down, do you really need all that ketchup, are you really going to wear those socks? Our pastor also encouraged Hillary to write an emotional autobiography, a personal will, and a letter to each of our children. She listened and calmed herself by deep breathing and repeating: 'Be Love. I am held in Loving Kindness. Trust Love. All will be well.' And then she wrote and wrote ..."

On hearing about Hillary's story and her writing, many grief group members initially felt awe and then regret that their deceased spouses or partners had not written letters. However, they quickly decided to creatively write what they thought their loved ones would have written. In so doing, they found and gave their spouses a voice and even expanded their own. The members realized that another can tell us what we don't know we know. The members not only supported one another but also unwittingly challenged each other to see freshly. At the last session, one member poignantly commented:

"I don't know about you guys, but I initially felt no connection to anyone here. Jerad, when you said you talked to stray dogs, cashiers, your mirror, and Martha, when you said with anger that your husband deserted you ... and Carmen, when you mostly just cried, I thought I was with a group of weirdos. As the weeks passed, however, I couldn't wait for our meetings—I love you guys. I can't believe how alike we very different people are! You all matter so much to me—my wife would die in shock [and he laughed] if she heard me talking like this."

Often people tell me about a surprise encounter that sparked a change in feeling and/or behavior. They describe surprise challenges, an argumentative neighbor's nasty comment, as well as surprise support, a friend's "warm" telephone invitation. After my own father's death, an ordinarily reclusive neighbor unexpectedly brought over a huge bouquet of fragrant lilacs. The flowers lifted my mood and connected me to my friend, to nature, to the Sacred, to God. I wrote this haiku:

Grief, like morning fog, had
surrounded and in-filled me.
Then I smelled the lilacs.

Whatever we lose—a spouse, a relationship, a way of life—we all need one another. Whoever experiences the losing—a senior citizen, a baseball player, a single business woman—we need one another. Many of us would probably agree with Dana: "Maybe separation is an illusion, maybe everything is interconnected ... everything exists because it is in relationship with something else ... it's all about relationships."

By creating community, by staying-in-the-conversation, we can find the strength to do the hard, deep emotional work that must be done if we are to continue living and growing after a profound loss. We may come to experience author Dr. Dean Ornish's belief that "we all have within us access to a greater wisdom, and we may not know that until we speak out loud." By really listening to ourselves and others, we can better understand both our unique story *and* the universal life story of losing and finding.

FOR MEDITATION
Sharing Our Story

"In hell, the people have chopsticks but they are three feet long, so they cannot reach their mouths. In heaven, the chopsticks are the same length, but in heaven the people feed one another."

—Vietnamese Story

"We only possess what we can give away."

—Simone Weil, Author

"When we think our sorrow is too great to be borne, let us think of the great family of the heavy-hearted into which our grief has given us entrance and, inevitably, we will feel about us their arms and understanding."

—Helen Keller, author

"Suffering ... anything borne by two is nearly a joy."

—Anonymous

"Somewhere, there are people to whom we can speak with passion without having the words catch in our throats.

Somewhere a circle of hands will open to receive us, eyes will light up as we enter, voices will celebrate with us whenever we come into our own power.

Community means strength that joins our strength, to do the work that needs to be done. Arms to hold us when we falter. A circle of healing. A circle of friends.

Somewhere, where we can be free."

—Starhawk, teacher

CHAPTER 4
Volunteering

Letticia was just leaving a neighborhood convenience store with fries, a shake, and a burger when some man approached her, begging for food. She told a group of us gathered at N Street Shelter for our monthly meeting: "No way did I want to share my planned dinner with this stranger. But I did. I gave him my burger and shake ... I wasn't ready yet to give him my fries."

Letticia continued: "I'm not forgetting that *I* lived on the streets for years and begged for lots of things. It was just around a year ago in late November that a stranger turned my life around. It was freezing cold and I was sitting huddled up on a park bench and a man stopped his car and offered help. When I told him to 'get-lost,' he urged me to 'stay-put.' He wanted to buy me some groceries. I wasn't going anywhere so, when he returned over an hour later with a sleeping bag, big warm coat, and 2 bags of good groceries—big oranges with no pits, I was still there and took the stuff. He also gave me a paper with the names and telephone numbers of three DC shelters. One was N Street. Three or four days later, I knocked on N Street's door and there began my recovery."

Letticia doesn't know what the stranger looked like and was pretty sure she never thanked him, but she did know this anonymous man's caring touched her profoundly. The stranger saw a need, felt compassion, and responded—with no strings attached. Many of us in this N Street Shelter circle of support commented on the man's spontaneity and his willingness to "put-himself-out" for a stranger. A woman from the group shared: "In an

A.A. meeting, someone said when we understand that most everything we have has been given to us, we're just more inclined to give too."

A humble appreciation for whatever gifts or talents we may have can stimulate a noticing of another's need. Compassion for anyone with a disadvantage leads to another spiritual practice—volunteering, a willingness to respond to a need when it arises.

Author Jim Wallis captured my heart when he wrote in *Who Speaks for God* about a news reporter's willing response to a need:

"A reporter who was covering violence in Sarajevo saw a little girl shot. The reporter threw down his pad and rushed to the aid of the man holding the little girl, helped them into his car, and sped to the hospital. The man said, 'Hurry my friend, my child is still breathing'… a while later, 'my child is still warm.' When they arrived at the hospital, the child had died and the distraught man told the reporter, 'I must go now and tell her father—he will be heartbroken.' The reporter said, 'I thought she was *your* child.' The man answered, 'No, but aren't they all our children?'"

This news reporter, the man caring for the girl, and the perfect stranger who helped homeless Letticia all noticed a need and responded. One such person in my own life was an older gentleman's large-hearted response to my request for directions. I was new on the job as a Hospice bereavement counselor in Washington, D.C., and atypically alone without my nurse or physician colleagues. A single mother had called, urgently wanting help settling a dispute with her terminally ill young son. I mistakenly thought I'd find my way (this is before cell phones and Mapquest). This older gentleman, who was chatting with a friend at a street corner, told me to wait a minute so he could get his car and lead me to my destination. He commented: "This is a bad neighborhood—there was a shoot-out between two teenagers in the area just a few nights ago. I'm not in a hurry. No problem. I'll wait for you and lead you out when you're finished—my pleasure." Another spontaneous angel?

Not long after, near the Washington Hospital Center, I had the opportunity to help a very confused lady find her way to the hospital to visit her very ill spouse. She had stepped off the bus at the wrong stop and had been walking up and down the "wrong streets" forever. It was such a joy to watch her high anxiety abate as she began to believe she would get to see her spouse before "he just slept." It was such a joy to see her husband weakly and gently pat her hand and stare lovingly at his befuddled, yet clearly loving, wife. It was such a joy to hold Lena's hand as she begged me to stay with her till her son arrived. It was such a blessing to witness the loving connection between two persons. Being a volunteer's recipient and volunteering ourselves—such real joy.

How paradoxical—the more we give away the more we receive. Friend Barbara Halpern believes the New Testament "Parable of the Talents" is about just that. Instead of burying our talent or gift, we multiply it by sharing it. The more we share our love, joy, wisdom, patience, courage with others, the more loving, joyful, wise, patient, and courageous we become. Goodness breeds goodness. A grieving man must have understood this when he told me: "Grieving persons like myself should close their doors, cross the tracks, and find someone to help—it's saved me."

In a support group, a newly clean addict, who was feeling unwise, unjoyful, and uncourageous, questioned: "What do *I* have to offer after living on the streets for so many years?" Someone quickly answered: "A smile. I like it a lot when Rawanda says my name, smiles at me across the room, saves me a seat; it makes me feel like I belong. It gives me hope to keep working the program."

Volunteering a smile can be transformative—whether it comes from a scared child finally calmed or a dying parent exuding loving acceptance of what is. Neighborhood friends like Evelyn and Jim are metaphorically smiling on the homeless at 7:00 a.m. every Sunday morning as they pick up day-old bread from local bakeries and then deliver the bread to area food banks and shelters. So many ways to "live-out" gratitude. Some commit to weekly tutoring at-risk children. Some advocate for affordable housing. Some take time to listen compassionately.

Wei Ping, a Chinese friend, tells me that the Chinese characters for the word 'volunteer' are: open heart, contribute your work [your gift], no pay.

Her definition reminded me of a Zen tale I read in college. A farmer found a beautiful rock, a gem, and was delighting in its glistening color when a traveling man came by and noticed the shining rock and wanted it for himself. He offered money. The farmer said: "No pay, you may have it— here, take it to enjoy." Not long after, the traveler returned saying: "You can have your gem back—what I really want is your ability to so freely give the stone away." The farmer would agree with Albert Schweitzer, who wrote: "One thing I know: the only ones among you who will be really happy are those who have sought and found how to serve."

Letticia was amazed at how happy she felt after giving away her burger and shake. Her A.A. sponsor had told her we are all continually breathing in and out. "We need to find that same rhythmic balance in our daily actions; appreciating all the ways we take from others and all the ways we can also share with them." Receiving and Giving. Both.

FOR MEDITATION
Volunteering

"I've come to believe that each of us has a personal calling that is
unique as a fingerprint—and the best way to succeed is to discover
what you love and then find a way to offer it to others in
the form of service, working hard, and also allowing the energy of the
universe to lead you."

—Oprah Winfrey, author, actress

"I slept and dreamt that life was joy. I awoke and saw that life was
service. I acted and behold, service was joy."

—Rabindranath Tagore, philosopher

"When you help someone take one step, Allah will help you both with
the next seven."

—Remla Kedir, a Muslim friend

"Do/give to other people as you would want them to do/give to you—
be compassionate. This is the core belief of every spiritual tradition."
—Joseph Campbell, anthropologist

"As with lovers,
When it's right, you can't say
Who is kissing whom."
—Gregory Orr, author

CHAPTER 5

Appreciating Coincidences

Friend Rita and other Hospice staff were concerned about Dan, a new patient who was very agitated. Many hours after Hospice admittance, the patient was still trembling and Rita remembered she had a CD in her lab-coat pocket, given to her by a colleague. She decided: "what-the-heck, there's a CD player here, I'll try playing the CD reading of T.S. Eliot's *Four Quartets*." Dan calmed down almost immediately and seemed to find peace in the reading. A few days later the patient died. A visiting friend, upon hearing the T. S. Eliot story, said with astonishment, "*Four Quartets* was his favorite poetry reading *and* Dan was a poet."

Paying attention to amazing coincidences and delighting in mysterious connections is another Spiritual Practice often leading to awe and thankfulness.

After hearing Rita's story, I wondered about adding another chapter on remarkable coincidences to *My House Burned Down And Now I Can See the Stars*, which had already been accepted for publication. Two weeks later, I was convinced. I was cleaning out a large desk drawer and found a toy angel that an acquaintance, Midge, had sent me thirteen years earlier upon hearing that our infant grandson had meningitis. The wind-up toy angel with fluttering wings brought smiles to our faces and an accompanying prayer brought some peace of mind. Soon after our grandson's rapid recovery, the angel was lost and Midge was diagnosed with an autoimmune disease. Our relationship was casual—she lived about an hour away and we had only met a few times at a monthly "Conscious Living" discussion group. However, as Midge's progressive illness was debilitating and she was more "home-bound," Midge's friend Joanne and I began periodically visiting her at home. Our friendship deepened—we were like college girls all grown up, discussing our husbands, romance, politics, our childhood, religion, our fears, life's purpose, death, books—everything. Therefore, when I found the angel, I was thrilled—I could now bring it over to Midge. However, upon calling, I learned from her husband Tom that he had just taken Midge to the hospital. Tom said Saturday would be a good day to visit. When we arrived, Midge was semi-conscious and dying. We prayed, were quiet; Tom sang and family gathered. Sunday morning, our vibrant, lovable, courageous Midge passed. Later that day, Tom asked me to speak, along with their grandson, at the funeral service. I immediately thought of the fluttering angel that so revealed Midge's generous, light-hearted, loving, and spiritual nature. Thank God, by coincidence, I had found the angel—just in time to show Midge's spirit to those gathered at the funeral, just in time to give *it* to Tom who, at the hospital, by coincidence told me with a soft smile that he believed in angels. Furthermore, I concluded my funeral reflection with a prayer, which Midge had loved when I had given it to her years ago. Several people in the congregation asked for a copy—two men saying: "it was just what I needed to hear." At the funeral luncheon, I told a fellow bereavement counselor about Rita's Hospice story and she told me about Dr. Paul Pearsall's book, *Making Miracles—Finding Meaning in Life's Chaos*. Years ago, this book had coincidentally also inspired my attentiveness to mysterious connections—inspired me enough to fill almost five journals with my personal examples of Serendipity / Coincidences / The Providence of God / Grace.

The night of Midge's funeral I remembered I had agreed to facilitate our Shalem interfaith prayer group meeting the next day at our home. I thought to myself: I'll just show a treasured framed print of Emile Renouf's 1881 painting, "A Helping Hand," and hope it's evocative for meditation. The artist's rendering of a beneficent old man-of-the-sea rowing and a tender little girl placing her hands on the oar with him is a captivating oil painting. I thought: possibly a meditation on trusting and going along with the flow. The fisherman could symbolize God, Father Nature, Wisdom, a kind old man. That night I checked my email before bedding down and a friend had sent the following Rumi poem, "That Lives in Us":

If you put your hands on this oar with me,
they will never harm another, and they will come to find
they hold everything you want ...

If you put your soul against this oar with me,
the power that made the universe will enter your sinew
from a source not outside your limbs, but from a holy realm
that lives in us ...

The poem was yet another serendipitous "Providence of God" coincidence that was appreciated the next morning by the group. Within two weeks, there had been so many wonderful examples of mysterious and miraculous connections.

As I write, I smile with the coincidence that I chose Albert Einstein's belief in a friendly universe and Psalm 139 to introduce this book. I smile with the coincidence that, soon after our first child's birth, Maschide's Zen saying: "My barn burned down and now I can see the moon" appeared in a book that I randomly chose for a birthday gift. That quote was just what I needed. As a new mommy, I was surely missing my mom. The quote reminded me that my dear mother's death gave me a new viewpoint—treasure every day, don't take life or others for granted, and look up at the stars and all that is given. How often I have subsequently quoted Maschide's saying to groups, at lectures, with clients, friends, and children. The enthusiastic response prompted me to consider writing this book about both feeling the deep sadness of a burned-down house *and also* choosing to look up and out for the bigger picture, the larger story. How could I not include a chapter on Providence of God, Grace, Serendipity, Coincidences, when I believe they are all over the place? How could I not share even another spiritual practice that transforms the heart and enlarges our world? How could I not share another practice that leads to deeper living and greater gratitude, humility, and hopefulness?

Finally, around this same time, acquaintance Martha Sherman, the finance director of Shalem Institute for Spiritual Formation, shared a story of coincidence. She felt so grateful to be part of the story of connections, she wrote her reflection for the Shalem newsletter:

"Commuting to work one recent morning, I was crossing the Metro platform, heading to the escalator, when I noticed a man on his knees on the ground, holding a bloody tissue to his nose. A loose circle of four or five others were standing around him but at some distance. Thinking he had plenty of help, I kept walking. But something gave me pause and so I retraced my steps and came to kneel beside him and offer him a fresh handful of tissues.

"As I knelt there, I noticed more details—a lot of blood on the ground, a man in a Metro uniform on his cell phone calling for help, a mother with a young girl about four years old who seemed very agitated as she looked from the man to the blood, two other women standing near and watching.

"As I continued to hand him handfuls of tissue as needed, a young man stopped and offered a suggestion to slow the bleeding. Someone dropped some pages of newspaper over the bloody mess on the ground. Another helped the man off his knees and into a seated position up against a wall. Yet another retrieved a shoe that the man had lost and helped put it back on his foot. The man on the phone kept trying to get some official assistance.

"I was struck by how each of us was doing one simple thing that all added up to this man being surrounded by care and getting the help he needed ... how simple it was really to be a helpful, compassionate presence in that moment and that I didn't have to do or even think of everything, only the part that was mine to do.

"As the man regained some composure, I asked him what had happened. 'I was crossing the platform to the escalator and I tripped over a KID,' he spit out—as if the child had no right to be there, as if the child were at fault for being only three feet tall and below his line of sight as he rushed for the escalator, as if the child had placed herself in his way and was the one responsible for this situation.

"I then realized that the young girl standing with her mother was the child in question. Recalling from my own childhood an experience of having been responsible for an almost-injury and the shame and mortification I carried for years about that incident, I pondered for a moment if I should speak to the child. Should I step even further into this situation? Was it presumptuous of me to assume I knew what she needed? I paused for a moment, asking for guidance, and the answer seemed to be, 'If not you, then who? (Coincidentally) who would know better how that young girl might be feeling right now?'

"So I approached the child and knelt beside her and asked, 'Were you hurt when the man tripped over you?'

"'No,' she answered.

"'Was it scary?'

"'Yes.'

"'Would you like to say something to the man?'

"With no hesitation, as if she were just waiting for the opportunity, she said 'Yes' and, still holding her mother's hand, she crossed to the man. I held my breath, hoping that the man would not growl back to the young girl, whatever she might say to him.

"With the man still seated on the ground, the two were at eye level with each other. Looking straight at him, she said gently and quietly, 'I'm sorry.' And he replied gently, 'I'm sorry.'

"And then the child reached her arms out to touch the man's shoulders and, leaning in, she kissed him on the forehead.

"And with the six of us others, now gathered closely around, I gasped. My heart swelled, felt too big for this body. I caught the eye of some of the others, and each seemed as moved by what we had just witnessed as I was.

"I will never forget that image of the child reaching her arms out to touch the man and kiss him with pure uninhibited Love.

"I floated on air the rest of the day as I recalled her stepping close and kissing the man. (I float on air writing about it now.) I could have simply felt good about stopping to help the man and accompanying him to his destination in case he needed help again. But, honestly, that was the easy part. We all do know how to help each other. I felt very blessed by Grace and Wisdom to recognize the child's distress and be guided to help her release her anxiety.

"But the abiding blessing of the experience, a blessing I am sure every person present felt, was to be witness to The Kiss. To witness—with simple presence—and in that witnessing, be so blessed.

"It awes me still ... that simply being witness to such sweet and pure compassion and love filled me full to overflowing ... so full of love that day that I think I could have flown if I chose to."

Buddha invites us to awake to all that is around us. The prophets in the Hebrew Bible and Jesus Christ in the New Testament invite us to see more clearly, and Mohammed invites the same. And what do we see? We may see and feel that the universe is friendly, offering great teachings when we see with the eyes of our heart. We may have a notion, as guest author Alice McDermott mentioned at our book club meeting, that God has an eye on the sparrow and the lilies of the field *and on us*. We may feel both an internal and external order and interrelatedness in our life. This recognition allows us to more freely change what we are able to change *and* accept what comes from a friendly universe beyond our control. Everything *does* belong.

FOR MEDITATION

Appreciating Coincidences

"We often dream about people from whom we receive a letter by the next post. I have ascertained on several occasions that at the moment when the dream occurred the letter was already lying in the post-office of the addressee."

—C. G. Jung, Psychiatrist

"Coincidence is the pseudonym dear God chooses when he wants to remain incognito."

　　　　　　　　—Albert Schweitzer, theologian, medical missionary

"Out of the welter of life, a few people are selected for us by the accident of temporary confinement in the same circle. We never would have chosen these neighbors; life chose them for us. But thrown together on this island of living, we stretch to understand each other and are invigorated by the stretching. ... We tend not to choose the unknown which might be a shock or a disappointment or simply a little difficult to cope with. And yet it is the unknown with all its disappointments and surprises that is the most enriching."

　　　　　　　　—Anne Morrow Lindbergh, author *Gift from the Sea*

"We are touched by what we touch, shaped by what we shape, and enhanced by what we enhance."

　　　　　　　　—Thomas Berry, Author

How to Recognize Grace

"It takes you by surprise.
It comes in odd packages.
It sometimes looks like loss or mistakes.
It acts like rain or like a seed.

It is both reliable and unpredictable.
It is not what you were aiming at
or what you thought you deserved.

It supplies what you need,
Not necessarily what you want.
It grows you up
and lets you be a child.

It reminds you that you're not in control
and that not being in control
is a form of freedom."
—Marilyn Chandler McEntyre, poet and author

CHAPTER 6

Forgiving and Asking Forgiveness

Many years ago I heard a story at "Common Boundary," a conference exploring the intersection of psychological and spiritual issues, that continues to invite reflection:

"One evening an old Cherokee told his grandson about a battle that goes on inside all people. He said: 'My son, the battle is between two wolves inside us all. One is Bad. It is selfish, argumentative, arrogant, angry, jealous ... and the other is Good. It is generous, humble, peaceful, serene.' The grandson thought for a minute and then asked his grandfather, 'Which wolf wins?' The old Cherokee replied gently, 'The one you feed.'"

Trying to understand some reasons for a negative behavior rather than condemning the person is feeding the good wolf. It's also a spiritual practice that encourages humbly forgiving ourselves and others for natural imperfections, poor choices, sometimes very poor choices, and fouling up in general.

As we grow wiser, we realize that focusing on another's negative behavior is often an easy distraction from focusing on our own—albeit, perhaps, more subtle darkness. When we are irritated with someone, we might practice centering and questioning, what is this resentment telling me about myself?

David's son Michael was seriously mugged near a shopping mall "by a teenage thug" who needed money for his drug habit. David felt as if his son was a powerless victim and felt more than resentment—he wanted revenge. David's rage toward the fifteen-year-old mugger was exacerbated when this mugger said dispassionately in court: "I just wanted his wallet, he wouldn't give it to me. I had to fight with him to get the money ... he was really fighting back." David became a victimizer, demanding that the arrested "brute should rot behind bars for years."

After too many restless nights and as many exhausting days, David finally agreed to talk to someone. Wanting to stop his internal battles, David began looking at and dealing with his self-righteousness, his obsessions, his capacity for hatred. He appreciated the Cherokee wolf story—he recognized his "bad wolf's" voice was overpowering his "good wolf." He eventually reflected and related in therapy:

"Under the 'right' circumstances, probably any of us is capable of committing pretty atrocious acts. ... Mike's many injuries blasted my world apart, blasted me apart—they're forcing me to see in new ways. I've been so oblivious to the desperation of the lives of inner-city youth. I had no idea a kid could live by himself on the streets right here in the nation's capital, having to steal to survive or, in this case, to support his addiction. My daughter, the psych major, tells me I'm addicted to being right, to money, to sports. ... It's a cliché, but I've lived a really sheltered life. ... He no longer seems sub-human but a victim also... God, we *are* victims *and* victimizers."

Several months later, David began a session by enthusiastically reporting his response to a radio program:

"Now I can—unbelievably—identify with Ronald Cotton. When Diane Rehm interviewed Ronald Cotton on National Public Radio, she suggested that he must be enraged for serving nine years in prison for a rape he never committed. Ronald answered that he was initially really bitter but, over time, decided to let go of his anger so he could make room for peace and grace.

"I can now imagine myself letting go of my anger to make room for peace and grace because I'm doing it. ... I've come back to life because I not only forgive the kid, but I forgive life! I re-found my heart. I can almost 'get' my friend who believes: 'Forgive them, they know not what they do.' I'm not furious at my wife for being so stuck in her anger. She's a good mother—devastated by our son's many problems. She can't understand me ... but I think I understand how her anger is covering over a deep, deep sadness and fear and vulnerability. I can't *yet* really console my wife but I've got to believe she'll eventually join me in leaving the past in the past and live in the present. ... I'm not forgetting, I'm just letting go, so regret and revenge don't overpower me, so I can find some peace."

David became a serious seeker who loved stories. He was especially moved by a story I had heard from an anthropology professor at a New York Museum of Natural History lecture years ago. In East Africa, a tribe's ancient custom gave the murdered victim's family the opportunity to choose the consequences for the captured murderer. Tribe elders loosely handcuff the apprehended murderer's arms and legs, row him out into deep waters, and push him overboard. The victim's family sits in a boat nearby and can choose to offer him a pole and pull him aboard, or let him sink and die.

The tribal teaching around these ancient practices is that letting the murderer drown may seem fair but it is reactive vengeance and doesn't encourage healing. Many of the tribe call this vengeance "a lazy grief." On the other hand, the victim's family that mercifully saves the murderer by finding a less torturous consequence most often heals.

David did not practice "lazy grief." He ultimately agreed with the more creative, less revengeful court sentence for his son's attacker. He gradually let go of his anger and then his profound sadness. He actually reportedly became a "bridge-builder" within his family when arguments arose.

However, David remarked toward the ending of therapy:

"My hardest work is still forgiving myself: regretting all the ways I wasn't there emotionally or physically for my son, particularly as he became a teenager ... would it have killed me to be a little more interested in his fascination with Stephen King and horror stories? If my son had died, I would have lost a son I had never really found! It's so hard at times to forgive Life for not turning out as I planned or wanted ... I can feel like I've been cheated. Forgiving is accepting all my dark, self-centered, stubborn, defensive stuff, and trying to change. I *am* accepting my daughter's idea that everybody is a work in progress. I'll never be quite the same."

Indeed, "letting go," forgiving, is a crucial spiritual practice. Emotional growth of adapting and seeing in new ways is impossible without forgiveness, whereas an open, loving spirit is possible with it. A "finding" is quite improbable without forgiveness, while new life and joy is quite probable with it.

A prayer found among the possessions of a Jewish man who died in a concentration camp during the Holocaust is an extraordinary example of finding new life after forgiveness. A minister read the prayer at a church service and the congregation's awed response was palpable. I and many others lined up asking for a copy. The prayer follows:

"Lord, when You come into your glory, do not remember only the men of good will; remember also those of evil will. And, on the Day of Judgment, remember not only the cruelties and the violence that they inflict on others; remember, too, the fruits that we have produced on account of the things they have done to us. Remember the patience, the courage, the sense of fellowship, the humility, the greatness of soul and fidelity that our executioners ended up awakening in each of us. Grant, then, Lord, that the fruits brought forth in us may serve also for the salvation of these men."

Letting go of reactivity and self-righteous indignation can initially seem impossible—as in the World War II example above. However, when we experience this large-hearted forgiveness, we witness its transforming effect. Letting go creates space for an awakening of courage and a "greatness of soul" within us. Letting go creates the space for reflective meditation, space for the centering practices proposed in each of the chapters of this book. With space and courage we can practice "Playing with Paradox," "Acknowledging Our Suffering," "Sharing Our Story," "Volunteering," "Appreciating Coincidences," "Forgiving and Asking Forgiveness," "Letting

Go and Lightening Up," "Opening to a Higher Power," "Looking Back," "Caring for Ourselves," and "Reflecting on Our Legacy." Choosing to make these practices habitual, we might agree with the philosopher Aristotle: "We are what we repeatedly do. Excellence then is not an act, but a habit." Finally, forgiving is life-giving. It's letting go of either/or, good or bad, black or white dualistic thinking and moving into the shades of color in between. We accept that within each of us there *is* both a "good wolf" and a "bad wolf," vying for our attention. We might begin imagining—inspired by the the Jewish victim of the Nazis—the awakening that can come from the other's evil. We might even choose to periodically say the following mantra as a way of feeding the good wolf while acknowledging the bad one.

I am loving kindness.
I care about myself and others.
I forgive myself and others.
I am loving kindness.

Forgiving and Asking Forgiveness

"Out beyond ideas of wrong doing and right doing
there is a field. I will meet you there.
When the soul lies down in the grass,
the world is too full to talk about.
Ideas, language, even the phrase *each other*
doesn't make any sense."

—Rumi, poet

"Ice and water,
Their differences resolved,
Are friends again."

—Y. Teishitsu, poet

"Evil, when we are in its power, is not felt as evil but necessary,
or even a duty."

-Simone Weil, author

"We can perceive ourselves and others as either extending love or
giving a call for help."

—One of the 12 Steps for Attitudinal Healing

"We had a fight and didn't speak
Wouldn't forgive, wouldn't be weak
We had a fight, don't know where to begin
But two hours later, we were friends again.
One scenario describes adults, the other children.
Whatever hurt was said or done,
hurt me, but I love you, I forgive you
And I'm walking away from it, not you."

—Tiffany, a bereavement support group member, spontaneously
wrote this after a discussion on forgiveness.

CHAPTER 7

Letting Go and Lightening Up

Years ago, while discussing the idea of living in the moment, Giles, a teacher friend, offered one of Abraham Lincoln's insights into human character: People are about as happy as they make up their minds to be. He asked his senior high students: "Do we create our own heaven, or our own hell? Do you agree with Lincoln that happiness is 'an inside job' rather than determined by external experiences?" His students initially disagreed with Lincoln. However, after a heated discussion many seniors did have examples of friends who had had lots of bad luck and were still "up" about life.

This choice of letting go and lightening up—of focusing on and looking for possibilities, 'the positive,' the humorous—can become yet another spiritual practice.

We *can* choose many of our responses—to feelings, people, and experiences. We can choose to smile. We can choose to patiently breathe deep. And we can choose to compassionately move away from sources of pain and emotional turmoil for the time being. We can "lighten up" and observe how life may be teaching us, working on us, and playing with us. We can also choose to focus with appreciation on what is given to us in the present moment, rather than just on whatever has been taken away.

Steve, a neighbor, had missed and grieved his deceased wife for months. He wanted to find "the joy in life again." Steve believed joy was an emotion of wholeness, and that joy occurred when he looked with appreciation at a "larger picture" of life. He loved a Bengali poet, Rabindranath Tagore, who wrote: "I slept and dreamt that life was joy/I awoke and saw that life was service/I acted and behold service was joy."

Believing that being awake and caring about others brought joy, Steve intentionally began "talking back" to some of his self-pitying interior voices. He wrote down and then daily read over his positive intentions:

"Be awake to right now. Appreciate the enoughness. Appreciate the abundance. Live in Loving Presence, forgive, live with love all day long. What happens to me is not anywhere as significant as how I choose to interpret and respond to the happening. Look for five things to be thankful for each day so I won't 'go down the tunnel'— *it's hard to be depressed when I'm being grateful!* Go to the Senior Center. Cross the tracks and be of service to the poor. Continually try new recipes and new foods to taste—and invite someone for dinner. Stock up from Trader Joe's once a week. Try new walking routes, and experiment with new words, saying them any chance I get. This week, 'bucolic'; next week, 'germane.' Here today, gone tomorrow; so play, work, share, and love today. The hardest years of life are between 10 and 70—and lucky me is 73!"

Encouraged by his daily written reminders and his chosen spiritual practices, Steve has been able to discover lightness and laughter almost everywhere. Reflecting on dying, Steve shared:

"When I'm finishing up on earth I'm going to have a thank-you party and give everyone a special note telling them how much they mean to me. I'll play the Beatles song, 'I'll Say Hello, You Say Goodbye.' Maybe I can get some fun ideas for a gravestone like: ' I never thought this would happen to me' or 'I told you I was sick.' At my party I'll ask for some of my eulogies, just in case there isn't an afterlife."

Steve was proud of and playful with his thrifty habits:

"I never waste time and money looking for another greeting card when I've already received one that has a great message. I just cross the original signature and put on my own—great recycling also. I got a card recently that on the outside said: 'This Message is Brought to you by the National Foundation for Lowered Expectations' and on the inside it said: 'Hope you have an Adequate Birthday.' How could I not re-use it? My daughter says I embarrass her but she really gets a kick out of my eccentricities. I think just watching life, the antics of squirrels ... and people, oh my God, just watching people, listening to birds, feeling the sun on your face is enough to make anyone smile. If we're not supposed to dance and sing, why is this music all around us?"

Toward the end of our work together, Steve brought me a Robert Bly poem and substituted Bly's words "a sad childhood" with his word "loss."

"If you had a sad childhood [loss], so what?
You can dance with only one leg
And see the snowflake falling
With only one eye."

A few weeks after concluding our grief work, I visited The National Gallery in Washington, D.C. and thought of Steve. Tibetan monks had worked contemplatively for three days at the gallery creating an intricate and colorful sand mandala. On the fourth day, they simply blew the great sand design apart, revealing to the audience their joy in creating and their acceptance of impermanence. Their smiles, joyful banter, and lightheartedness were contagious.

Are we ever far from finding fascinating and unexpected twists in life, finding both inspiring and annoying people, or life's generous offerings? Frequently coincidences can enchant, funny movies offer delight, and authors may inspire. And, of course, our embarrassing personal blunders and our humorous stories are ever with us, to elicit a laugh if we so choose.

Dal, a friend of forty years, had learned, as Steve had, to enthusiastically live a passionate and participatory life. He was born in Sri Lanka and loved his life, his family, and America. When he was critical of greed, consumerism, militarism, and secularism, many people took his remarks seriously, but not personally. His energy, his ability to laugh, and his underlying gratitude for all of life drew listeners into his campaign to resolve and reform conflict. We felt challenged, not criticized. Four years ago, at age 76, Dal was diagnosed with stomach cancer. He continued to focus on whatever was possible and positive. His wife Theodora told us, "there's a certain delightfulness in him that can't be hampered." Dal took time to create a "new normal," a new good. A good meal was anything his tiny stomach would tolerate. An exciting weekend was being able to stay awake for his visitors. A wink, a touch, a prayer, hand-holding, and beautiful music were all cause for deep appreciation. He died living. He died loving. He died the way he lived. He was ready to be companioned to a new way of living. He felt his aches were labor pains readying him for a birth into fuller love, into his God's embrace. He went not-so-gently physically *and* gently emotionally into that good night. He reminds me of the writer Dr. Seuss, who believed fascinating people and fascinating experiences are "here, there, and everywhere."   Albert Einstein, similar to Dr. Seuss and Dal, embraced a friendly and teaching universe. Einstein answered "Yes" to his important question quoted at this book's beginning: "Is the universe a friendly place?"

Embracing a friendly universe, we practice remembering how frequently day follows night, sunshine follows rainstorms, and new forms of animal life and vegetation follow volcanoes. Seeds of our life are cultivated with the compost—the refuse—of our daily experiences. We can choose to be noticers of the whole story.

Finally, in the midst of a loss we can feel *both* sad *and* hopeful, *and* perhaps even grateful and lighthearted in anticipation of an upcoming surprise.

FOR MEDITATION

Letting Go and Lightening Up

"Humor is the prelude to faith and laughter is the beginning of prayer."
—Reinhold Niebuhr, philosopher

"Life must be lived as play."

—Plato, *The Laws*

"The joy that isn't shared, I've heard, dies young."

—Anne Sexton, author

"When the trees sing,
  It doesn't really matter
If you know the song,
Or if you know the words,
Or even if you know the tune.
What really matters is knowing
That the trees are singing at all."
                    —Mattie Stepanek, a teenager undergoing treatment
                                for a rare and fatal disease; author

The Party

"We were all invited
to the party. Children came

Lots of children.
Singing
Clapping
Smiling
Reading
Laughing.

And grown-ups, too

Sharing stories

Telling secrets

Joking
Dancing jigs
Holding hands.

We threw confetti

Whirled and twirled

Hopped and skipped

Hugged and hoped

   it would never end.
Then she stepped out
Of the crowd and said:
"I've got to go."

We huddled together
   Stopped the celebration
   And said
"No!"

   She said
   "I'm sorry
   but please
   don't stop the
Party just because I'm leaving."

   And then she turned her
         face
   to the moon and
         stars
   and lifted her arms
         up wide
   and shouted
   "God, What a party!
   Thanks so much
       For inviting me."

   And then she looked at us

and smiled

     and, turning, waved,

     and walked into

     the night."

        —Joan Fleming (written for her friend, Hospice patient
        Kathy Rushing—when Kathy was dying)

CHAPTER 8

Opening to a Higher Power

When a friend from the Midwest called to tell me about a tragic mother-child auto accident, I felt an empty pit in my stomach. I had just heard recounted most mothers' worst nightmare. Several weeks later, this same friend shared the extraordinary dream of Jenna, the grieving mother. I felt some relief. Jenna had accidentally and tragically run over and killed her only daughter, Mari. Her daughter had been riding her tricycle as Jenna backed the car out of their long, curved driveway. For months, Jenna was beside herself: guilt-ridden, traumatized, and numb. Around five weeks after her daughter's tragic death, Jenna had a transforming dream. The dream transported her to another realm, to Mystery.

Choosing to humbly open up to another realm, to "a power greater than my own," is a Spiritual Practice. Connecting with the God of our understanding—for many a personal and loving God—often gives deeper meaning and purpose to life.

In Jenna's dream, daughter Mari came through the bedroom door with a boy about a head taller than she. Mari very lovingly stroked her mother's leg and said something like, "Mom, we are O.K. I'm here with Craig and we're fine, really fine ... don't worry." At that moment Jenna awoke in amazement and shock and quickly awakened her husband. Who was this Craig that her daughter presumed she knew? Her husband suggested they call their friends who had a neighbor named Craig. These friends had brought Craig with them when the two families had gone camping the previous Labor Day weekend. Jenna did call. Their friends reported that Craig had died four or five days earlier of leukemia.

Jenna subsequently wondered, "How could this be—is it true that my dreams work to bring me back to balance? How could my unconscious know that Craig had died? Maybe it's true that Mari and Craig are just in another form of energy." She felt compelled to share her healing dream with anyone who would listen. She felt an invisible hand guiding her and was told by her pastor about Psalm 15: "Even at night He gives me counsel." Jenna felt God was not only a noun, but a verb pulsing life and love into all of creation—the heart of everything. God was becoming less about a belief and more of a felt relationship—an "I/Thou" meeting with Mystery and Presence. She loved and found great comfort from and connection to the words of Chief Seattle of the Suquamish Nation, who reportedly spoke in 1852 about the "behind the scenes" love, order, and wholeness of creation:

"Every part of this earth is sacred to my people. Every shining pine needle, every sandy shore, every humming insect. All are holy in the memory and instinct of my people. We know the sap that courses through the trees, as we know the blood which courses through our veins. We are part of the earth as the earth is part of us. The perfumed flowers are our sisters. The bear, the deer, the great eagle are our brothers. The rocky crests, the juices in the meadows, the body heat of a pony, and man all belong to the same family."

Diana, another grieving mother who initially felt isolated and disconnected, eventually became not only connected to other grieving persons but also connected to a loving sustaining Presence she found around and within herself.

Diana shared her "Waking-Up to Life" story with friends at lunch. While returning home from college for summer vacation, Diana's son's car had been almost totaled by a speeding car that had collided with her son Will's old VW "bug." Diana's son lived, after enduring almost a year of pain, various therapies, and difficult legal battles. On the first anniversary of her son's accident, Diana saw a bald eagle soar over her neighbor's trees early one morning. She wondered if God had sent it to her. She wondered if this was a gift to lead her to more peace. But then she wondered: "If God *did* send an eagle, why didn't He stop drunk drivers?" Actually, Diana had lots of questions. She walked. She walked some more. She read. She particularly appreciated the author and mythologist Joseph Campbell's findings: From time immemorial, cultures have carved out some sacred space. From time immemorial, myths reveal a basic trans-cultural belief of available support, internally and externally, from a Higher Power. Myths recurring across cultures dealt with Diana's questions: "Why does the Creator allow suffering, free will, evil?" "What's the point of it all?"

After a year of grief work (feeling and adjusting to her son's diminishments, reading, discussing, counseling), she felt new. For Diana, the one-year life-giving anniversary gift could have been glorious yellow chrysanthemums, a compassionate neighbor offering a meal, a friend volunteering with her at MADD, or ... a bald eagle.

Her anniversary gift also could have been an interior one of peace, recollecting the words of mystic Julian of Norwich: "Winter comes and goes, all will be well, all manner of things will be well, this I know." Or it could have been hearing Apollo Astronaut Captain Eugene Cernan's remarks to a National Public Radio interviewer: "What I saw was just too beautiful to have happened by accident."

However, for Diana, her stated greatest gift was a growing desire to know God by cultivating an awareness of love—or the possibility for love—in all her encounters. She appreciated Rabbi Jonathan Sacks' belief that one cannot let go of a grief until one has found a blessing in it. She practiced noticing blessings in the give-and-take of life.

Diana appreciated a mysterious thrust toward balance, imbalance, and return to balance repeatedly occurring throughout the universe. Diana began to trust that day follows night—over and over again. Somehow fledgling Arctic terns who have been orphaned in the northern climes know how to locate the nest of their parents half a world away in Antarctica. No one understands exactly how terns do this. The earth knows to revolve around the sun. Squirrels know to bury acorns for winter. To spawn, salmon and sea turtles know to swim back to the precise places where they were born. Even ice "knows" when to melt and peaches "know" when to ripen. Leaves "know" when to fall. There is a glorious, knowing energy that pulses throughout the universe. This energy inspires the ivy to conceal our garages and grow through cracks in the pavement, and inspires hydrogen to combine with oxygen to form water. This energy connects the tides to the moon, the bees to the flower, and the daffodils to spring.

With eyes, ears and heart wide open, each day holds revelations, new invitations. Just watch NOVA on a Public Broadcasting Station, take a walk, gaze. The wild geese, the gently falling snow, the flooding storm waters all speak a sign language that we can choose to learn. Diana agreed with author and theologian Karen Armstrong that our own self-preoccupation keeps us from living with more awe, keeps us from a relationship with God. Discovering that at the center of every major spiritual tradition is the injunction to be compassionate toward everybody, Armstrong writes: "Compassion asks us to dethrone ourselves. Our own egotism keeps us from God."

Seeing freshly, planet earth invites all to see with Elizabeth Barrett Browning that:

"Earth's crammed with heaven,
And every common bush afire with God;
and only he who sees takes off his shoes;
The rest sit around it and pluck blackberries."

With shoes off, we can learn, as the Chinese farmer's neighbor did (p. 9), that everything seems to belong and everything conspires to teach us that creation is *ultimately* friendly. Even if we creatures cannot understand, we can begin to trust and watch for the signs of new life springing forth from the aftermath of an earthquake or from a "dead" tree, from a job loss, or from a failed marriage. This is the life, death, and rebirth circle. This cycle of both losing and finding in all of nature can lead us to deeper forgiving, trusting, and caring. Again, losing is only part of the journey, the part that needs to happen for us to believe "that somewhere in the darkest night a candle glows."

Songwriter Irvin Graham believed: "for everyone who goes astray, someone will come to show the way." Perfumed lilacs, soaring birds, beautiful music, being valued, giving and receiving warm smiles, a tender touch—something or someone will come to show the way. We might just take off our shoes, even if the sand is hot or the garden is muddy, and stand on sacred ground.

We may notice that, if we had never suffered and grieved our losses, we might not have a sense of the holy, we might not have been as curious about the unanswered questions, we might not even have asked questions. The questions invite pause and keep us humbly awake to Mystery, which theologian Karl Rahner, S.J., says is another name for God.

At the end of one of our bi-monthly Women's Group Gatherings, we especially felt this sense of Mystery after we had each shared a favorite poem. A friend Julie captured the moment by reading the following prayer and poem by Frederick Buechner:

"The way the light falls through the windows.
The sounds our silence makes when we come together like this.
The sense we have of each other's presence.
The feeling in the air that one way or another we are all of us here
    to give each other our love, and to give God our love.
This kind moment itself is a door that holiness enters through.
May it enter you.
May it enter me.
To the world's saving."

As we make space for the kind moment, we can actively choose to practice an openness to *both* the ordinary *and* the mysterious. The kind moment can become "a door that holiness enters through."

FOR MEDITATION
Opening to a Higher Power

"We all worship at some shrine; find the most authentic."
—Simone Weil, author

"Our responding to life's unfairness with sympathy may be the surest proof of all of God's reality."
—Rabbi Harold Kushner

"Wherever you turn, there is the face of God."

—The Koran

Question to Dorothy Day, author and social reformer:
"Do you really believe in God?"
Answer to a college student:
"Whom do you say thank you to?"

—Dorothy Day, spoken at a NYU 1966 workshop

I Believe

"I believe for every drop of rain that falls, a flower grows. I believe that somewhere in the darkest night, a candle glows.

I believe for everyone who goes astray, someone will come to show the way.
I believe, I believe.
I believe above the storm the smallest pray'r will still be heard.
I believe that someone in the great somewhere hears every word.

Every time I hear a newborn baby cry, or touch a leaf or see the sky,
Then I know why I believe."

—Written by: Irvin Graham, Jimmy Shirl,
Ervin Drake, and Al Stillman

CHAPTER 9
Looking Back

Believing that life is lived forward but understood backward, a visiting German psychiatrist at my school said in an early 1960s lecture:

"Regularly look back on your lives—extract value from your experiences. If Goldilocks looked back over her past month, she'd recognize she learned faith and perseverance from visiting the three bears' home. She kept trying to find the right porridge, right rocking chair, and right bed—she kept working things out. Same for Hansel and Gretel ... they found together they had unimagined courage to fight the witch-wickedness. Journey *through* life's difficult experiences— discover the hero within. Dorothy on her journey to Oz found she had a tender heart, courage, and wisdom all within her—just waiting to be practiced. By not journeying through life's difficult experiences, we usually become stuck, addicted, and un-heroic! Often the undealt-with life-challenges lead to misery and addictions. Dealing with problems leads to liberation and satisfaction ... and often faith."

Believing that our life journey and others' life journeys yield golden treasures to be mined, it behooves us to periodically look at our history from a new perspective. Choosing to grow, become more whole, and see freshly evokes this spiritual practice.

Around five years ago, while cleaning out stashed-away graduate school notebooks, I happened upon the above notes from the psychiatrist's talk. I had forgotten about the lecture, forgotten the psychiatrist's name, and only vaguely remembered loving the lecturer's accent, his love of fairy tales, and his witty engagement with his audience. It was now, looking back, that his words really resonated with me. Similarly, it is now that poet John Keats's writing to his friend resonates with me: "Do you not see how a world of pain and suffering is necessary to school intelligence and make it a soul?"

Awakening to a deepening consciousness, both respect for our own history as well as respect for others' histories grow. The word "respect" comes from the Latin word spectare—to look. Re-spect invites a "looking again," perhaps a little deeper, with a less reactive glance. A re-looking reveals that the mud does indeed settle to the bottom and that the muddy water does eventually becomes clear.

Carol, a grief group participant, did this "re-looking" after participating in our Hospice parental loss support group. After the last meeting, she shared some written reflections with me:

"I *can* resolve to be more accepting of my losses: I *can* resolve to keep in touch with my feelings about them. But can I resolve such a mysterious and profound happening? I think I will always wonder about the loss ... when my daughter turned two, it struck me deeply that I was her age when my first mother died. Suddenly, if I were to die, she would have no memory of me and our times and our love, just as I have no memories of that time with my first mother. That realization was hard. I began to keep an occasional journal, asking all the while, why did my mother not write to me? Surely she knew she was dying; her diagnosis was two years before her death. Why didn't she preserve some memories, write a letter, make her love more tangible?

"Now, coping with the loss of my second mother, my outlook has broadened. With the help of the group, I began to question ... maybe my first mother could not accept the idea of leaving behind such young children. Maybe when she accepted the reality of her impending death, there was too much fear or pain or indignity to make room for MY eventual reactions to her loss. It was maybe not so much a matter of ignoring the depth of my loss, but of her need to concentrate on her own reaction to the inevitable. These recent losses allowed me to revisit the earlier one, and bring a new perspective to it. I may never 'resolve' my losses, but as each new experience of loss comes, I am dealing better with it."

Carol revisited losses as well as wrote a letter to her deceased biological mother, mentioning both what she appreciated and didn't appreciate about her reputation. This writing helped treat a wound. However, even though Carol grew in her understanding and appreciation of her biological mother, it again didn't mean there wasn't a wish that it could have been otherwise.

Remembering and honoring her deceased parents, grief group participant Kathy Williams wrote these two poems:

"Iris"

My mother was no iris
purple and regal
head held high for admirers,
bold, frilly, and headstrong.
Not my mother.
Though my garden holds her iris,
old-fashioned and small-headed,
though I painted them in watercolor to hang on her wall,
though Van Gogh's note cards acknowledge the condolences;
my mother was no iris.

My husband says a white calla, but I say peony.
She was more the blown white peony.
White hair full around her pink Irish face,
head heavy bent with time
and ready to leave after the next storm,
to scatter and brown and return to the earth
after so brief a lightness.

Old-fashioned and simple.
Her tangled roots resistant to transplanting,
treasured for quiet beauty,
gone just as I breathe closely the fragrance
of that childhood garden memory.

"Parting Gift"

Silence was the norm
between "my country right or wrong" father
and the art-school hippie
I had become.

I want to show you something, he said.

I followed the path of his heavy shoes
out into the meadow
to witness the silent dignity of a box turtle
as she carefully positioned herself
and deposited her leathery eggs
in the hole she had prepared.
I ran back to the house for my camera.
My father squatted in his gray work clothes
and had a smoke to mark the occasion.

I am older now than he was then.
Did he also carry that solitary, sweet memory
to glisten in his mind until the end of his days,
fresh as those wet and waiting turtle eggs?

Ahh, so much connecting—whether a mother to a peony, or a father
to a daughter: "I want to show you something," he said. Digging deeper
into our personal gold mine of memory by writing poems, journaling, and
reflecting on past experiences and relationships invites awe. We notice
again and again the interconnectedness of all things. We might unpack
our heavy suitcase often overburdened with accumulated reactions to life's
challenges. We may choose to travel light. Less encumbered by feelings of
resentment, loneliness, and anxiety, we have space in which to behold all
that is given right now—in the present. Traveling lighter and living with
the possibility in the present, we realize: nothing risked, nothing gained.
Unburdened, we're willing to try something new—a grief group, and even
an imagination exercise within the grief group.

Because imagining the comments of an estranged friend or deceased person can lead to untouched depths in our memories and more creative, in-the-present living, I ask support group participants to go to the beach and sit, "eyes-closed," by a sand dune to visualize the chosen person. After being-with the ocean waves and blue sky overhead, feeling the sea breeze, the caress of the sun and soft warm sand, participants eventually meet their deceased or estranged "loved one." I then ask each group member to "imagine what that person and you want to say to each other."

Participants are sometimes surprised by their new and unexpected feelings and by the reassuring words they hear. Often there is cathartic crying. We can become emotional just imagining the sound of our mother's voice summoning us home on a summer evening with: "Yoo-hoo." One teary woman smiled and shared: "I heard my mother singing ... 'button up your overcoat, when the wind is free, take good care of yourself, you belong to me.'"

Many participants openly "discuss" an unsettled concern with the imagined deceased person and move towards a more complete resolution of conflicting emotions or unhealed wounds. Many realize that even the selfish, grouchy, arrogant behavior of those long gone can actually be an invitation to choose a more compassionate response. Every experience, every person, can be a gift for us both emotionally and spiritually, and often that gift reveals its different aspects at various stages of our lives. One group member said to me after a Let's-Imagine-Meeting: "Shit, before this exercise, I would have imagined my know-it-all father giving me advice. Just now I did experience his giving me advice but I felt he was quieter and there was worry and caring behind the advice ... and I imagined high-fiving him and it felt great."

Those who revisit past losses sometimes discover that they never lose what they love deeply; for what we love *does* become a part of us. Cherishing our memories through rituals can give us a sense of continuity and connection with the past and perhaps even diminish our fear of death. We see death as the dance partner of life—it is part of the rhythm. Living with our mortality, we can become more alive in our living—we don't have forever. We learn that most people die the way they live. So, right now, we practice living more generously and lovingly—letting go of our pride and sharing our vulnerability and tender heart. We ask for or give forgiveness, discuss a secret worry or embarrassment, ask a conflictual question, express our love or need for love. This is a part of our life work, our grief work. And perhaps, as Thornton Wilder suggests, "The greatest tribute to the dead is not grief but gratitude." And remembering. And living and loving more deeply *now*. And honoring the ordinariness and extraordinariness of the life we share.

Rituals such as this "We Remember Them" reflection by Jack Reimer and Sylvan Kamens invite remembering:

"At the rising of the sun and at its going down
We remember_____

At the blowing of the wind and in the chill of winter
We remember_____.
At the opening of the buds and in the rebirth of spring
We remember_____

At the blueness of the skies and in the warmth of summer
We remember_____

At the rustling of the leaves and in the beauty of autumn
We remember _____

At the beginning of the year and when it ends
We remember _____

As long as we live, they too will live, for they are now a part of us,
As we remember_____

When we are weary and in need of strength
We remember_____

When we are lost and sick at heart
We remember_____
When we have joy we crave to share
We remember_____

When we have decisions that are difficult to make
We remember_____

When we have achievements that are based on theirs
We remember_____

As long as we live, they too will live, for they are now a part of us,
As we remember_____ "

Often this reflection is read after a family gathers, as a candle burns on the anniversary of the death of the deceased who would be sitting in the empty chair. After reading the above reflection, those present can share memories: "Remember how Dad always wore that beat-up old Yankee baseball cap that mom hated, remember how Mom always asked if we remembered to write a thank-you note to Uncle Harry?"

Those present can later create an "I remember" memorial booklet about the deceased which can include photos, stories, favorite quotes, sayings, special recipes, favorite heroes and heroines, favorite books, and movies. Many grieving adult children wear a deceased parent's bathrobe or favorite tee shirt; a friend savored drinking out of her mom's old chipped mug that had been a mother's day present years and years ago.

Everything that happens to us is part of the chapters of our life story. Our current chapter is built on our first chapters of life with our parents and significant others; so those now absent are not here—and yet, very much here, with both their positive and negative influences.

Therefore, whether we look back like Carol, through her above written musings about her mom or like Kathy, through her above poetry about her parents, the remembering itself can so enrich the present. Contemplating behavior patterns that we've learned from our family of origin helps us choose which behaviors to keep, and which to not keep. It is never too late to discard any masks we may have acquired and live closer and closer to our true self.

Additionally, does not reviewing the grand richness of past experiences, fairy tales, cycles in nature, a research project, joyful, scary, sad times, our varied relationships help us appreciate the depth of our life experience? Perhaps as we become more awake and appreciative of living, we'll be more able to celebrate the greening of spring and "let go" when autumn comes. Possibly we can agree with theologian Richard Rohr:

"There is a certain fear of death that comes from not having lived yet. I had to face it myself when I had cancer a few years ago. I don't think I was afraid of death at the time, but I also knew that I had already lived! Once you know you have touched upon the mystery of life, you are not afraid of death. There is an existential terror about losing what you've never found. Something in me says, 'I haven't done 'it' yet. I haven't touched the real, the good, the true, the beautiful—which is of course what we were created for.' When we know we have experienced it, we will be able to lie on our deathbed like St. Francis and say, 'I'm not afraid to let go of life because I have life, I am life. I know life is somehow eternal, and another form is waiting for me.'"

During the first few decades of our life, we write our story. During the following decades, we can pull together the story and write the commentary—"what was that all about?" Psychoanalyst Erik Erikson asks if we can ultimately find meaning in our life dance. He asks if we can accept our life progression—the process—rather than continually lament over missed opportunities or goals. Rumi suggests this progression in a poem:

Little by little, wean yourself.
This is the gist of what I have to say.
From an embryo, whose nourishment comes in the blood,
Move to an infant drinking milk,
To a child on solid food,
To a searcher after wisdom,
To a hunter after more invisible game.

Are we willing—now—to play around with the life that seems to want to live in us? Can we shed all our early wounds, our old skin so as to wean ourselves *and* let ourselves be mysteriously weaned? What are we feeling called to emphasize? David R. Hawkins in *Reality and Subjectivity* believes: "To become loving brings an end to the fear of loss of love, for lovingness engenders love wherever it goes." This belief goes right along with the Biblical verse 1John 4:18: " ... but perfect love casts out all fear."

Looking back, we might find revealed examples of this truth so that now we might choose to practice loving deeply more often.

As we weave the disparate threads-of-life together into one meaningful, grand life tapestry, hopefully we can really taste the unique, love-filled, and amazing life that is ours or can be ours.

We probably will notice that we "grew up" after facing a severe winter that required some hibernating, some plan-changing, and some losing. Somehow, barrenness leads to fullness, winter leads to spring, death leads to life over and over again. Leaves have died into soil for new trees, tree limbs have died to give birth to the fire, candle wax has died to become light. Glaciers have died to become water. Everything is eternally leaving and returning.

Even the beech leaf, upon "reflecting" backward, can "notice" the great cycles and circles in life:

"And, oh, the quiet of pond ripple
And cumulus cloud;
The quiet of wooded ground life,
And the still music of other dried, yielded leaves
Carried by the subtle Autumn breeze.

I let go past Winter, but am not finished—
Like generations before me,
Am becoming soil for new greening."

—Anonymous

Periodically we choose to practice reflecting on our journey of living through both Fall and Spring. We discover, repeatedly, that when something is taken away, something else is given. We live in possibility as we *both* harvest memories *and* plant new seeds.

Looking Back

"Remember what you have seen—for what is forgotten returns on the circling wind."

—Black Elk

"Men go forth to wonder at the height of mountains, the huge waves of the sea, the broad flow of the rivers, the vast compass of the ocean, the courses of the stars; and yet they pass by themselves without wondering."

—St. Augustine, *Confessions*

"Until I just shared all these stories from my past I never realized how often I do the same dumb things I did as a child—I'd withdraw when my mom was clearly favoring my brother or just not listening to me. Now I do the same withdrawing when my husband seems to favor his work over the family—I hurt myself over and over again and keep expecting different responses than I got as child ... I set myself up because I'm afraid of conflict ... I'm now seeing how my past has conditioned me ... and I don't have to keep living that way."

—Barbara, friend

"Nothing goes away till it has taught us what we need to learn."

—Pema Chodron, author

"We shall not cease from exploration
And the end of our exploring
Will be to arrive where we started
And know the place for the first time."

—T.S. Eliot, "Little Gidding," in *Four Quartets*

CHAPTER 10

Caring For Ourselves

Many years ago at a school playground, a mother asked the seven-year-old son of our friend: "What does your mother want most this Mother's Day?" He answered: "To go back to bed." The assembled parents enjoyed a laugh, but we recognized that he spoke close to the truth. While we all agreed we could use more sleep, none of us was curious enough to explore solutions to our common dilemma. We just bemoaned our fatigue and bragged about all we had to do.

During this young period in our life, my friends and I were busy living our life-story and didn't take much time to reflect on how healthy, holy, or whole (words from the same old English root, Hal) we were. We simply showed up to the day and did what we imagined we needed to do.

However, as we grow older and wiser we become more curious about how we are balancing our mind-body-spiritual needs—an essential spiritual practice in caring for our deeper soul needs. This balancing act is one more practice that energizes our life-spirit and values each individual life.

Following his dog Lightning's death, everything seemed to stop for Henry. In the process of grieving his beloved dog's death, Henry's organized world began to fall apart. He was too often tired, "gray," and out of balance. His come-out-and-play companion was gone. He sat for hours with himself and unexpected memories and vulnerable feelings began to surface. After many months of feeling passively depressed or aggressively stubborn and explosive, he listened to a dog-loving colleague's suggestion: "Talk to someone!"

In one of his early therapy sessions, reflecting on his marriage, Henry reported:

"Without Lightning to distract me, I've noticed how barren our marriage has become. God, we've BOTH been like children, each wanting our own way ... each waiting for the other's invitation to play. Instead of fun playing we resorted to playing tit-for-tat, often trying to get back at the other. I'd put my cap on the kitchen doorknob and she'd put it in the hall closet, then I'd get it and put it right back on the doorknob. One rainy day as she was leaving for a baby shower, she threw the hat out the back door and she screamed that I was like a child and that it was good we didn't have children; a child can't be a father. Then she left crying and we both didn't talk until her cousin visited on the weekend. We were cool and cordial. Her cousin started asking questions and I heard Helga say that I was impossible, that I didn't even know her ... *all* because I told her to have a good time at a friend's baby shower. ... She also said that I'd eventually want sex, so I'd then pay her some attention, as if nothing had happened."

Henry continued:

"After her cousin left, I felt bad and was extra helpful. And much later in a conversation I told Helga that we had both collected grievances, both been bitter about our inability to have children, both blamed each other. ... I suggested that her digestive problems and my insomnia were symptoms of something...they say our bodies don't lie. We cried together, and man, it felt great—we were at least doing something together." (They loved it when I shared that in Chinese, according to friend Dr. Wei Ping, the word "good" is comprised of two characters, one is a "boy"and one a "girl." The Chinese evidently knew thousands of years ago that, for something to be "good," there needed to be a balance of *both* masculine *and* feminine energy.)

Months later, during a joint session with Helga, Henry agreed that he had been responsible in his job and in tending to sick relatives. He believed he had *not* taken care of his spiritual needs by joining Helga in her spiritual community or finding his own place to worship, his own place to "stop and be, stop and connect with something beyond himself." He had *not* taken responsibility for his emotional need for intimacy. Henry said to his wife poignantly: "You know what I really want from you? It's not sex, or money from your job, or to be right: it's to feel valued and respected!" As he freely shared his ache, he agreed with poet Emily Dickinson that: "A death blow is a life blow to some." They both agreed that they had tumbled around with Lightning more and more and less and less with each other. Now it could change.

Like houseplants that reach toward the sunlight to care for themselves, so too Helga and Henry, by slowing down and working in therapy, reached toward their own unique source of light. They noticed their soulful needs had been left by the wayside during their keep-busy life. They now stayed in comfortable *and* not-so-comfortable conversations. Grieving their dog's death *and* the distance in their marriage had become a door-opener, inviting a deeper quality of presence to their pain as well as to all of life. They both were inspired by Buddhist Tara Brach's suggestion that below all our turmoil is a quiet space of healing and liberating presence—a refuge. Each learned to live with an open heart and a "Beginner's Mind"—as discussed by Vietnamese monk Thich Nhat Hanh in *The Miracle of Mindfulness*, one of Henry's favorite new books. He "coined" his own fresh word: "heartfullness."

In a word, Henry was curious. The word 'curious' comes from the same Latin root as the word 'cure.' In therapy and in his reading, Henry was on the lookout for paths leading to improved self-care, to good health. Henry's curiosity was contagious. Helga joined him in engaging in life *and* in stepping back and reflecting on: "now what is this about?" Helga and Henry both found that their curiosity led to cures. They moved from "Yes ... but" to "Yes ... and" people. Futhermore, they were open to additional self-care pursuits such as gardening, discussing feelings, physical exercise, and listening to music, as well as opening to their dreams. Examples follow:

Gardening invites stillness and a temporary time-out from grieving. One neighbor who had recently lost her husband said: "When I go out to my garden, all my senses wake up. Gardening, like all nature, is both predictable and not predictable—joining me with the larger rhythms and cycles of life. ... I get caught up with tomatoes and basil, living stuff; I see plants as metaphors for *us*. We grow and give life, we need pruning, cutting down, transplanting, watering, nurturing, and we, like any good perennial, regularly die, but regularly come back to life!" A friend said to me: "Gardening reminds me: *we* don't grow the plants but we enable the growing by planting seeds and preparing soil. The Spiritual Practices you suggest are about planting seeds and preparing our soil so growing can happen."

Physical *exercise* produces energy. An elderly widow and neighbor laughed: "I need my daily morning walk to lift my spirits, to connect me to myself and to others, and to energize me for the day ahead!" Mattie, a Yoga classmate shared:

"With Yoga, my body becomes more resilient, as does my spirit. The consistent deep belly breathing and stretches have saved my life…'Child's Pose' places me in a position of healthy humility; 'Warrior Pose' is empowering, balancing, and stilling, and 'Sun and Moon' salutation connects me to a larger world. Concluding with 'Corpse Pose' invites surrender and total relaxation. And then I love ending class with a gentle bowing to the sacred in one another with the word 'Namaste.' As the physical balance of opposing forces (effort and surrender) happens in Yoga, a spiritual practice of balancing opposite feelings (assertion and passivity) in my emotional life is happening as well. … I love Yoga."

Healthy Eating leads to healthy living. Consider: more spice, less sugar; more water, less soda and coffee; more fish and vegetables, less red meat; more greens, more fresh fruits and produce, less refined salty foods. *Particularly* if we are grieving, avoiding alcohol and sugar—both depressants—suggests responsible self-caring. We are what we eat, we are what we practice.

Music can tap into the full range of feelings we might experience in response to life's losses and challenges. Gerald, a fellow we met in Bay St. Louis, Mississippi, doing Hurricane Katrina relief work, shared:

"Singing 'We Shall Overcome' gave us strength during our civil rights marches…church spirituals sustain us through life's sorrows and connect us in faith and happiness also. I don't know how I'd survive without music ... anywhere I go I tap my feet, get some rhythm going. So many moods to music like so many moods for us. When I sing at a funeral service, I can actually feel sad and joyful at the same time."

Discussing feelings and simultaneously sorting out the many layers of a loss or a conflict is another aspect of good self-care. Ruth talked with her childhood friend and then with me in therapy. She had felt lonely for several years, had a poor relationship with her mother and no boyfriend who "stuck around." She said: "Everything I do is halfhearted." She worked hard at opening up to a close friend and to me in therapy and eventually invited her mother to join her in a therapy session. Perhaps they both could live with less resentment.

At the first mother-daughter session, Ruth asked her mom if she could discuss a fifteen-year-old, festering wound. Receiving a nod, Ruth proceeded:

"When I was around ten years old, I ran into your bedroom in the middle of the night terrified by a horrible nightmare. You shooed me back to my bedroom without giving me any comfort, and then in the morning Tom, Jeffrey, and I had breakfast and you never asked me a question about the dream or my fear before I went to school. You seemed more interested that we finish our oatmeal."

Until this moment, neither her mother nor Ruth had ever discussed the nightmare incident. However, Ruth's mother did remember that night of years ago and shared with emotion how scared and sad she herself had felt that "nightmare evening." After a long pause, her mother said:

"Prior to your bursting into the room, your dad had reported how fed up he was with my preoccupation with you kids. He felt I was often too tired to pay attention to his needs for connection. I, of course, had wanted to respond to you the night of the nightmare, but was afraid dad would see it as another rejection, just when we were becoming close. When you seemed okay the next morning, I didn't want to upset you again by reminding you of the dream, or upset the breakfast right before school; also I didn't want to go into detail about our marital issues with you. I think you were only about ten."

Assumptions checked, Ruth now viewed her mother as *both* sensitive *and* insensitive. Her mother was human! And so, too, was Ruth. Good self-care, for Ruth, now also entailed living in a broader "both/and" world. Her mother had *both* failed her *and* blessed her.

Journaling focuses. Nancy, a member of Alcoholics Anonymous and a grieving wife, wrote about her journaling experiences for me:

"I don't know how deeply I feel about something until I let the words or even sometimes a sketch flow onto the page. I reread my journal jottings regularly so as to remember what has touched my heart—what I'm thankful for daily and what's 'stinking thinking' that needs some correcting. I write down lots of A.A. slogans (like what we resist, persists,) and then I confront something I want to avoid. Simply, A.A. saves my life from the first step of declaring my Powerlessness to the need to forgive and help others.

"Journals are a safe place to store my 'yahoos,' my irritations, anxieties, inspirations, thoughts, whatever. ...Journals are my place for letting all my junk anger hang out (what you call grieving). Recording my big feelings of rage toward my daughter Judy, who is still smoking despite her dad's death from lung cancer, literally is saving my relationship with her. Once I named my feelings on paper and sat with them—rather than telling her what an unbelievable idiot she was—these feelings no longer overwhelmed me. Journaling is helping me get at the root of the negative emotions I'm experiencing before acting impulsively. ... Journaling reminds me I have an inside balancer."

Additionally, journals can become wonderful old friends that can "visit" with us in our more senior years and remind us of our life adventures and forgotten feelings.

Attending to our dreaming, to the stories woven from our unconscious each night, is another practice opening us up to our deeper selves. Psychiatrist Carl Jung believed that: "When we do not pay attention to our dreams, it is like getting a letter from God and not opening it."

After a divorce and recent surgery, Ester, in therapy with me, shared a life-altering dream:

"I was reading and developed stomach pains which were becoming intolerable. I called my mother who lived nearby and asked her to take me to George Washington University Hospital. When she came, music was blaring in the car and it really annoyed me. I also felt annoyed that my nephews were bumping into me as they wrestled in the car. My mom hit the curb and drove fast over potholes, so I felt bumped around by the ride. Upon arrival at the hospital, I jumped out and angrily slammed the car door and ran into the emergency room. Then, I woke up—annoyed."

As Ester discussed her dream, she realized that her unconscious was inviting her to "deal with conflict." Initially, she thought the dream was prompting her to "quit depending on my clueless mother." When Ester said that she had no further comment, I suggested that, if it were my dream, I'd wonder why I hadn't asked my mom to turn the radio down and drive more slowly over potholes, and why I hadn't asked my nephews to stop wrestling. If it was my dream, I might be fascinated that at the end of the dream ...

Ester immediately exclaimed:

"That's me. I say little when upset but later explode and then mom or my ex calls me a lunatic; I slammed the door with hostility without having verbally expressed any of my needs."

Her dream awakened her to her "either passive or aggressive" pattern and her fear of conflict. Now she tries to be moderate and assertive.

Poetry is a deepening activity. Carol Peck, whose father died in our Hospice program, believes that writing poetry simply keeps her alert.

Carol believes we access our vulnerable feelings when we compare our beloved deceased person to a particular animal, fruit, color, sound, smell, force of nature, texture, taste, emotion, or feeling. She has learned that such metaphors, comparisons between our loved ones and non-human creatures or things, help us see them in new ways that ultimately broaden our consciousness.

Elaine H., a grieving daughter, wrote about her dad, a Holocaust survivor, a metaphoric poem:

"My first thought is that he was like a storm,
Loud and demanding and cruel at times,
Which then blew over and was all serene,
Except for the damage he left behind.
My first thought is huge and wants to crowd out
Whatever else I've known or glimpsed,
Of sentiment and poems of love,
Of hair curls saved, and babies' footprints.

I think now he was more like a faceted stone,
And somehow, along the way,
I missed out on the facets on which the sun shone,
And now I'll miss them till the end of my days."

Poetry can be cathartic as well as focusing. While at the hospital with his dying dad, our sons' friend Derek Thurber wrote this poem about the possibilities inherent even in the act of dying:

"Isn't it great to be alive tonight?
Your mind's eye can look back
Like a descending sun reviews clouds.
Your own eyes can look brilliantly
Upon the faces of your children, your wife.
Dying, you gain powers.

The sun burns unbelievably red,
Seems to immolate the earth
In what really amounts to a promise:
Lending us fire for the night.

Father, you have found your clouds.
You have given your gift.
All we can do is receive
your warmth and your fire
like once we received
your arcing footballs."

Meditating and praying quickly brought balance to our neighbor Khaled, a fast-talking, high-achieving CEO. An elderly woman sitting next to Khaled on an airplane overheard two of his frantic cell phone conversations before take-off. In an ensuing conversation, she advocated his calming down or "his tongue would make him deaf." Appreciating the grandmotherly concern, Khaled agreed to read her suggested Thomas Keating book on centering and meditation.

Khaled told me:

"My new commitment, sitting still most mornings, breathing in and breathing out 'love' or 'peace' or 'patience' have brought me home, not only mentally, but physically and spiritually as well. I'm listening more to others, to nature, to my heart … to all my senses. I'm *here*, now. I breathe like I'm connected to the basic drumbeat of life, to Allah the Source of all life. I'm not creating the silence, it's within me all the time; I enter into it as I watch a bird fly, a leaf fall, children absorbed in play. I enter into silence when hiking in the woods, while walking in the snow, visiting a cathedral, gazing at stars, when watching a sunrise at the ocean. Meditation for me is not so much the absence of thoughts but a detachment from them, so there can be an opening to something more, something larger than my little world. In the solitude I feel both separate from and connected to all of life. Meditation frees me from me. By letting go of my grip, I can flow with life."

He laughed one day as he told me that his wife wanted the workaholic back—she had lots for him to do. He reported: "I try to coopereate with my wife and also keep faithful to my multi-faith practices—I particularly like beginning my day sitting still in our walk-in closet with a Celtic chant:

Deep peace of running wave in me,
Deep peace of the quiet earth in me,
Deep peace of the flowing air in me,
Deep peace of the shining star in me,
Moon and stars pour their healing light on me.
Deep peace,
Deep peace of the Creator Spirit in me.

Fortunately, claiming these self-care practices as well as the practices mentioned in each of the preceding chapters graces us with intellectual, physical, and emotional energy. This energy enables us to do our grief work as we come to terms with our loss. This energy awakens us to the day before us, awakens us to surprise gifts revealing themselves in the friendly universe all around us. This energy invites action—we choose to smile at others and at ourselves and our body feels the goodness.

When we choose to *both* step into life wholeheartedly *and* step back to rest, learn from, and listen to Life, we are active *and* contemplative. *We care and we don't care.*

FOR MEDITATION
Caring For Ourselves

"The Chinese characters for the word 'busy' are, killing/ severing the heart."

—Robert Sutter, George Washington Univ.
Professor of Chinese Studies

"Those who contemplate the beauty of the earth find reserves of strength that will endure as long as life lasts."

—Rachel Carson, author

"Plant a green tree in your heart and perhaps a singing bird will come."
— Chinese proverb

"Let yourself be silently drawn by the stronger pull of what you really love."
—Rumi

Slowing

An overcast day,
grass and tree, my chair atop a rolling hill of farmland.
A tiny washed-out yellow butterfly,
intoxicated with weed and warmth,
pirouettes quickly from wild flower to wild flower.
I want to say, "Please stop.
Sip some lemon-grass tea.
Drink in the brilliant orange and various shades of growing green;
hear the mourning dove greet the new day with distinct song.
Soak up the smell of horse and grain, wild rose and honeysuckle;
let the at-once timid and quite assertive breeze play with you."

The butterfly is just being a butterfly;
It is I who want to sip tea.
—Ann Hisle

CHAPTER 11
Reflecting On Our Legacy

After fleeing their homes as the 30-foot waves approached, many victims of Hurricane Katrina in Bay St. Louis, Mississippi, related how keenly aware they became of what they valued most. Letters, photos, souvenirs, family stories were their treasures. They became stunningly conscious of what had given meaning to their lives, what touched their hearts, and what could wash away. Isn't this a question for us all?

Wanting to share our life-learnings, our unique personal legacy, our ethical will, our accumulated wisdom is a spiritual practice that reveals a generativity and generosity of spirit.

Reflecting on our legacy requires being attentive to purposeful and accidental threads and themes we've woven into the fabric of our lives. Are not the lessons we've learned part of the collected wisdom we've gained from one choice leading to another choice throughout our adventure of meeting life? Does not our wisdom come from letting life work on us, play with us, teach and love us?

Hopefully we observe and embody wisdom that we want to share— this passed-down wisdom often takes the form of a written document, a personal will, a memoir to accompany our legal will.

Months and months before Hillary's death she had begun collecting her wisdom. She had let life work with her, she had accepted her pastor's and then husband Bruce's suggestion that she write her own personal will so their daughters could sustain a connection with her. Bruce had pleaded: "write about what matters to you ... tell them why you decided to marry me and some of the arguments you had with your mother about me." He had reminded Hillary to let her heart speak to the girls. While in conversation one day, Hillary reportedly laughed: "I have more good stuff to share than I ever imagined. They won't have to presume so much because I'm giving them concrete vignettes." Hillary not only shared her emotional autobiography but also practical suggestions such as her favorite recipes, books ... and guidelines for a good husband: "Watch how he treats his mother and odd-duck kind of people, how kind he is to beggars, how willing he is to say sorry and mean it."

Hillary believed her young daughters would probably want to know her more as they matured. She wrote letters for each daughter's sixteenth birthday and wedding day.

After Hillary's death, Bruce reported in a partner-loss support group that he believed his wife's writings would be life-saving treasures for his daughters. Years later, I telephoned him and he reported: "In five months, my youngest daughter will be sixteen and I will be giving her a personal letter from Hillary describing her values, her remembrances of this daughter during her younger years, and her appreciation of and hopes for her. With indescribable joy, my older daughters have read and re-read the letters—one proclaimed the letter to be the most treasured inheritance anyone could receive."

Audrey, a widow of a former Hospice patient, also was guided by the remarks of her spouse his last weeks on earth. His legacy: "You need to reach out—you've depended too much on me and the kids. Now you have to ... become yourself." She was depressed and stopped by her husband's recent death and also stung by his leave-taking words. After mostly home-bound months of staring into space and mulling over her life and her husband's admonitions, one morning she decided to tune in to National Public Radio. It just so happened that a Chilean peasant mother of a murdered son was being interviewed and asked to comment on the atrocities of the former Pinochet dictatorship in Chile. The grieving mother said slowly: "Pinochet's men can kill our youth but they cannot stop Spring."

She suddenly felt her husband was speaking through this mother to her. She had to move from winter into spring. Feeling so awed by the grieving mother's faith, Audrey ventured out to the library, to the grocery store, and then to the ice cream shop. When she returned home, she called me and left this message: "Please call me ... I think I'm crossing the bridge ... I was on my way home from shopping and was hot and hungry; I stopped and got a Cherry Garcia ice cream cone and it tasted good. My taste is coming back."

Soon after listening to Audrey's message, I re-wrote a haiku:

Grief, like evening fog, had
Surrounded and in-filled her,
then she met a Chilean mother
and "Cherry Garcia."

A week later Audrey volunteered with a neighbor at the library to help tutor immigrants needing help with their English and registered for an upcoming exercise class. Her "I'm not going to bother" transformed into "No harm in trying!"

Living a daily "*yes*" to the day and taking some risks with new relationships was Audrey's gift to herself and would become her legacy to her children. Audrey's choices revealed: it's never too late to rewrite some life scripts. Choosing this "yes" and noticing the kinship between losings and findings throughout life's recurring seasons may be akin to Rumi's invitation to be a searcher ... "a hunter of more invisible game." This searching and noticing invites us into a friendly universe and a friendly universe into us.

As we celebrate our searching, our "Aha" moments, the insights that have made our life particular *and* universal, we may want to meditate on or write about our ethical/personal will to include:

- Heroes, people, experiences that have influenced me.

- Who has touched and is now touching my heart? Who have I touched?

- Do I have an image that reminds me of precious time when my heart opened?

• Mistakes that became gifts.

• Favorite books, movies, songs, holidays, games, favorite foods, recipes, TV shows, vacations.

• Favorite quotes.

• What matters to me?

• When given a day off from work, what is my idea of a good day?

• Embarrassing, funny, frightening, exciting, frustrating, and transforming experiences.

• Changes that I adjusted to—and changes that I didn't adjust well to.

• Joys of my life, sorrows of my life.

• Opportunities—and, perhaps, missed opportunities.

• Truths life has taught me.

• My contributions to family, friends, neighborhood, various communities to which I belong; my contributions to the lives of others.

• What are the events in my life that seemed random when they occurred, but now seem to be part of a coherent whole?

• What did I come to earth to learn, to heal, to love?

• Write or find a quote, a poem, a Bible passage that reveals wisdom, a type of wisdom that both inspires and challenges me by giving meaning, perspective, and an example of a truth that I embrace.

The above reflections, as well as some of our own favorite writings, can be part of our unique written personal legacy. Here are some examples I include in such a will:

"How
Did the rose
Ever open its heart
And give to this world
All its
Beauty?

It felt the encouragement of light
Against its
Being.
Otherwise,
We all remain
Too
Frightened."
   "It Felt Love," by Hafiz (14th c.)

"Love is the cure,
For your pain will keep giving birth to more pain
until your eyes constantly exhale love as effortlessly
as your body yields its scent."

                             —Rumi

"This is what the Lord asks of you,
Only this:
   To act justly, love tenderly, and walk humbly with your God."
                          —Old Testament, Micah 6:8

"Love is patient, love is kind. It is not jealous, it is not pompous, it is not inflated, it is not rude, it does not seek its own interests, it is not quick-tempered, it does not brood over injury, it does not rejoice over wrongdoing but rejoices with the truth. It bears all things, believes all things, hopes all things, endures all things. Love never fails ... So faith, hope, love remain, these three; but the greatest of these is love."
                —New Testament, I Corinthians 13:1-9

If I focus on living with faith, hope and love, will I not see, along with writer Paula D'Arcy, that God comes to us disguised as life? Will I not see light and love in a lady bug, a cleared path in the woods, in water raining down into a flowerbed?

"God's joy moves from unmarked box to unmarked box,
from cell to cell. As rainwater down into flowerbed.

As roses up from ground.
Now it looks like a plate of rice and fish,
now a cliff covered with vines,
now a horse being saddled.
It hides within these,
till one day it cracks them open."

—Rumi

Ah, how good it is when we have inward eyes to see so much life in a plate of rice and fish, in a soccer kick, in a smile, an ant colony beneath a rock, a horse being saddled. Ah, how good it is when we have The Chinese Farmer's compassionate detachment (p. 10). Ah, how good it is when we are awake when the sun does rise and when the sun does set—and ultimately can give thanks for it all.

Student: What can I do to become enlightened?
Zen Master: As little as you can do to make the sun rise.
Student: Then why do you suggest spiritual practices?
Zen Master: So you are awake when the sun does rise.

FOR MEDITATION
Reflecting On Our Legacy

"One day we'll learn that death cannot steal anything gained by the soul."

—Rabindranath Tagore, poet

"Let life be as beautiful as summer flowers, and death be as beautiful as autumn leaves."

—Rabindranath Tagore

"This is how we know
we are no longer hungry … that
the world is full of terror, full of beauty
and yet we are not afraid to find solace here.
To be bread for each other. To love."

—Gunilla Norris, "Plenty"

"This is ancient wisdom from my native village in China: When a young person is leaving home pursuing his or her life, the elder's legacy shared in Chinese characters translates as: *Stay hungry and foolish.*"

—Ms. Wei Pin, M.D., friend

"I abandon all that I think I am, all that I hope to be, all that I believe I possess. I let go of the past, I withdraw my grasping hand from the future, and in the great silence of this moment, I alertly rest my soul."

—Howard Thurman, *Deep is the Hunger*

"I believe unarmed truth and unconditional love will have the final word."

—Rev. Martin Luther King, Jr.

"We are what we repeatedly do. Excellence then is not an act, but a habit."

—Aristotle, philosopher

Before an omen arises,
it's easy to take preventive measures.
What is still soft is easily melted;
What is still small is easily scattered.
Deal with things in their formative state;
Put things in order before they grow confused.

—Tao Te Ching (500 B.C.)

Like a caring mother
Holding and guarding the life
Of her only child,
So with a boundless heart
Hold yourself and all beings.

—Buddha

"Birth is a beginning
And death a destination.
And life is a journey:
From childhood to maturity
And youth to age;
From innocence to awareness
From ignorance to knowing;
From foolishness to discretion
And then perhaps to wisdom;
From weakness to strength
Or strength to weakness—
And often back again;
From health to sickness
And back, we pray to health again;
From offense to forgiveness,
From loneliness to love, from joy to gratitude,
From pain to compassion,
And grief to understanding—
From fear to faith;
From defeat to defeat to defeat—
Until, looking backward or ahead,
We see that victory lies
Not at some high place along the way,
But in having made the journey, stage by stage,
A sacred pilgrimage.
Birth is a beginning
And death a destination.
And life is a journey,
A sacred pilgrimage—
To life everlasting."

—Rabbi Alvin I. Fine

After a friend, Annalee Oppenheimer, read the manuscript of *My House Burned Down and Now I Can See the Stars*, she sent me a copy of her deceased mother's 2013 Christmas letter, written 10 weeks before her death. Her mother gave her life away—it wasn't taken from her!

Annalee wrote:

"… She did not have it easy—she had been wheelchair-bound for 17 years before she died. Five of those years she lived alone in her home after my father died.

Reading her letter—a legacy—always makes me feel close to her because it shows how she approached life. For example, she attended tai chi class up until the last week of her life. She was not able to stand due to a balance problem and she could not lift her arms very high because she had chronic pain in both shoulders, but she could breathe—and so she enjoyed following the class by breathing along with everyone else as they did the tai chi forms."

Christmas 2013

My ninth great-grandchild was born this past year. Other than that, my life has been uneventful and that very un-eventfulness is newsworthy. At 91, the fact that I enjoyed a year of good health is not to be taken for granted.

"Live life well" is the motto of Westminster-Canterbury. I have lived well this year. My worldly possessions are whittled down to fit into one room. While paring down my possessions was difficult at first, I now feel that the simplicity of having only a roomful of things to keep track of is liberating. I have the run of a beautiful building with libraries, parlors, and dining rooms that are someone else's job to maintain.

My daily life is full of activities that nourish me physically, mentally, socially, and spiritually. Benedictine monks believe that a balanced life should include five practices: labor, study, hospitality, renewal, and prayer. Upon reflection, I realize that my daily life includes all five practices.

At my age, propelling myself from place to place in my wheelchair and keeping on top of the logistics of life require enough physical and mental energy to count as "labor." While I don't have a formal course of "study," I read voraciously and am always learning new things in my Bible study group, book club, and the lectures offered here. Visits with family and friends offer ample opportunity for "hospitality." I experience renewal through making pottery, going to musical concerts, and trips to the thrift shop in the basement. Finally, my day includes private "prayer" and I regularly attend Evensong and healing services in the chapel. This chapter of my life feels more simple, balanced, and prayerful than the busier, more frenetic chapters of my youth.

And yes, there are challenges in this chapter of life. Living in a long-term care means that I am up close and personal with death and diminishment. Sadly, on several occasions this year, I learned of the unexpected death of another resident with whom I had been chatting only hours before he or she died. These experiences have reminded me that every human encounter is precious, and now I try to be more present in my routine interactions with everyone.

In the dining room, I often see a man tenderly spoon-feed his mother. It takes an hour and a half for her to complete the meal. I feel blessed to see what genuine love looks like in a very intense and specific way. Every day I see many examples of this type of love in action here.

I realize that our diminishments provide opportunities for qualities such as steadfastness, kindness, patience, and fidelity to come forth. Our physical reality by its very nature is full of heartbreaking limitations, but it is the hard edges of these limitations that allow us to experience the *unlimited* divine love and peace available to us.

May you experience God's unlimited love, joy, and peace in 2014.

Bernice Flynn
Westminister-Canterbury

My Personal Story of Losing and Finding

I remember playing "sailboat"—holding my handkerchief out the car window as we were driving to my grandparents' home. I was around five years old. Suddenly, the blue and white "sail" slipped from my grasp and my father immediately noticed, saying, "That's what happens when you play around." I didn't dare ask him to circle back and retrieve my handkerchief-sail. My decent, sensitive, and strict father didn't like carelessness and I felt ashamed. Some months later, I lost a treasured flower pin and I was again quickly reminded to stop fussing. I didn't dare cry about my loss or sulk over my father's annoyance.

At a young age I often emulated my father, who did not appreciate displays of negative or vulnerable emotions, but who did appreciate a "stiff upper lip" mentality. Consequently, at age 17, when my mother was diagnosed with lymphoma cancer, my script was in place: help with the housework, support my mother, try to keep my dad in a good mood, do not complain. When my mother died several months later, a philosophy was already in place: "Your mom is in a loving community in heaven. Be thankful for having a good mother for so many years. Accept what you cannot change." I worked hard to push my pain away and hush my upset. I did not feel entitled to feeling sad and "sorry for myself" since I had learned well that whatever was could have been worse. So I cried by myself and felt guilty for being so self-absorbed and ungrateful.

After my mother's death, there were times I both couldn't and didn't distract myself from three visitors: sadness, jealousy, and loneliness. I remember well one summer day, as my eighteenth birthday approached, being drawn to the water at a quiet local beach. It was a weekday as I lay on the beach, atypically alone, not distracted with friends and activities.

Lying still in the warmth of the sun and the sand, I began to cry, to sob. I felt heavy and molded in the sand below. My first birthday without my mother was in a few days, and I felt empty and alone. Eventually, I got up to swim. It seems like yesterday: the choppy waves, the blue sky, the sailboats, the clarity of it all. As I swam slowly past the long stone pier and bobbing floats, I felt cradled as I was carried along, like a child's leaf-boat floating easily, quite surrendered, in the salt water. My heart connected me to something much larger than myself: the Long Island Sound feeding into the Atlantic. Somehow I felt connected to the waves of life, to my mother, to my ancestors, and to God, the loving, life-animating Source of all that is.

I felt *both* sadness *and* gratitude and began tearing again, this time with a sense of the sacred. As I remember that day, a Wendell Berry poem comes to me now:

"I come into the presence of still water and I feel above,
day-blind stars waiting with their light.
For a time, I rest in the grace of the world and am free."

All of a sudden, I had felt a presence and a connection that took some of the sting away from my mother's physical absence. I actually began talking to my mom inwardly and imagining her response. I was beginning the practice of *Acknowledging and Allowing my Feelings*, and staying with them.

After that morning at the beach, I began to awaken to the *paradox* that it was in the presence of death that I began feeling deeply the miracle of life. I began to awaken to the paradox that I could feel *both* sad and isolated early in the morning *and*, an hour later, feel peaceful and connected.

It was several years later that I found another finding. After the birth of our first child, my husband John encouraged me to spend hours and hours *sharing photos, stories, and feelings* about my life with my mom. It was during the *story-sharing* that I remembered, made conscious, and embraced my dear mother's *deep faith and her connection with God*. Her faith guided her throughout her illness and her dying. I remembered her appreciation of Reinhold Niebuhr's prayer: "God give us grace to accept with serenity the things that cannot be changed, courage to change the things which should be changed, and the Wisdom to distinguish one from the other." [Worn copies found in her top dresser drawer and her purse].

Looking back over the years as John and I were raising our four children, I realized the profound influence of my mother's death. Make today count. Notice the extraordinary in the ordinary: hand-holding, smiling, listening, sharing an ice cream soda. Her loss led me to be more sensitive to others' losses and led me to my chosen career. Remembering my mom's saying: "this too shall pass" inspired a *lightening up and a letting go*. Remembering my mom's injunction: "Be careful about making snap judgements of others —we often don't know the whole story," inspired a growing *forgiving of life, myself, and others.*

Additionally, around this time of children-raising, I was nourished by Zen poet Masahide's haiku—"My barn burned down, now I can see the moon"—which in my mind I changed to "my house burned down, now I can see the stars." This quote put into words an intuition I had had on-and-off since my mother's death. I kept being re-amazed at the profound truth of the inexorable partnership of apparent opposites. Quaker author Parker Palmer suggests a partnership of humility and chutzpah. Oscar Wilde writes of our early need for success, followed by needed failures to awaken us. Spiritual author Barbara Brown Taylor asks, "What can light possibly mean without dark?" I hope I am letting both the losings and findings, actually, the whole of life, both work on me and play with me—internally and externally. If I am upset, I try to get myself outside and connect with my upset and connect with all the love, turbulence, and life in creation. That's when I seem to come to my senses and *let life give to* me. Just the smile to and from a stranger, the smell of cut grass, and a rain storm are all life-giving; and each is not just a "just." I feel seeds of deepening trust have begun to sprout as I slow and watch, as I become more and more drawn into silence. There a healing and life-giving grace pops into my head, a written thought or feeling touches my heart; another's loving kindness inspires faith, hope, and love. Anything beautiful, like fragrant lilacs, enchants me and calls me to another place and reminds me that everything speaks of the glory of God. So much reminds me of Albert Einstein's belief that "Yes," the universe is fundamentally friendly.

Now I'm aware of making a circle, returning home to my beginnings, with a new appreciation of my need for both my mother's receptive silence, her praying, her self-sacrificing, and her humble being, her acceptance of what cannot be changed, her bowing down; as well as appreciation of my father's judging and his proactive participation in external pursuits, his standing up. Being naturally more active and extroverted, I had lost my mom's appreciation of contemplative silence. Gratefully, by balancing my two parents' philosophies, I have found both "introversion" and "extroversion" living together within me.

My parents gave little heed to *self-care*; this has been a new teaching for me. I've learned: "You have to take time to fill your own water jug if you want to have water to share with others." I learned this from John, my friends, and from nighttime dreams revealing my need for pauses, silence, prayer. I had subsequently thought this was selfish, a luxury—the last twenty years it has become more foundational.

Taking or making time to *look back* over my personal life *and* my life work of counseling and teaching has been a rich experience and will be part of my *personal will*. What an honor to be invited to accompany so many on their heroic journey into the *underneathness* of their own lives, the underneathness of life itself. What an honor to watch attention shift "from my fears, my smaller life, into expansive life." What an honor to intentionally greet each morning with: "May I love well today" and watch others do the same.

The spiritual practices discussed in the preceding chapters have befriended, strengthened, and healed me, and others on our journey, to *both* deeper humanity *and* deeper divinity. They keep reminding me and others of the ever-present life force of Love (for me, God in all things) and the teachings of nature. The practices help us experience the amazing hopefulness and resilience within our own human spirit. They invite us to stay lovingly awake, live gratefully in the miracle of Presence and be teachable—intentionally participating in the progression of weaning and maturing.

The spiritual practices suggested in the preceding chapters hopefully enhance our maturing, our life search into deeper loving, into wisdom, balance, and the "invisible game." They help us recognize the magic of being alive—enabling us to see and respond to the "good" and "evil" of life … and accept uncertainty and loss. We have hope of *a finding*!